Standard Grade | General

Biology

General Level 2004

General Level 2005

General Level 2006

General Level 2007

General Level 2008

Leckie×Leckie

First exam published in 2004.
Published by Leckie & Leckie Ltd, 3rd Floor, 4 Queen Street, Edinburgh EH2 1JE
tel: 0131 220 6831 fax: 0131 225 9987 enquiries@leckieandleckie.co.uk www.leckieandleckie.co.uk

ISBN 978-1-84372-620-3

A CIP Catalogue record for this book is available from the British Library.

Leckie & Leckie is a division of Huveaux plc.

Leckie & Leckie is grateful to the copyright holders, as credited at the back of the book, for permission to use their material.
Every effort has been made to trace the copyright holders and to obtain their permission for the use of copyright material.
Leckie & Leckie will gladly receive information enabling them to rectify any error or omission in subsequent editions.

BLANK PAGE

[BLANK PAGE]

FOR OFFICIAL USE

G

KU	PS
31/49	35/41

Total Marks

0300/401

NATIONAL
QUALIFICATIONS
2004

WEDNESDAY, 19 MAY
9.00 AM – 10.30 AM

BIOLOGY
STANDARD GRADE
General Level

Fill in these boxes and read what is printed below.

Full name of centre

Town

Forename(s)

Surname

Date of birth
Day   Month   Year

Scottish candidate number

Number of seat

1 All questions should be attempted.

2 The questions may be answered in any order but all answers are to be written in the spaces provided in this answer book, and must be written clearly and legibly in ink.

3 Rough work, if any should be necessary, as well as the fair copy, is to be written in this book. Additional spaces for answers and for rough work will be found at the end of the book. Rough work should be scored through when the fair copy has been written.

4 Before leaving the examination room you must give this book to the invigilator. If you do not, you may lose all the marks for this paper.

SCOTTISH
QUALIFICATIONS
AUTHORITY

1. (a) The diagram below shows a food web from a woodland ecosystem.

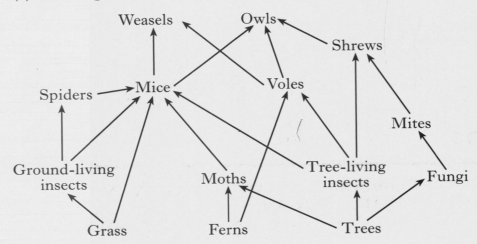

   (i) Complete the table below to show each consumer from the food web and its diet.

Consumer	Diet
Mice	spiders, ground-living insects, grass, moths, tree-living insects
Moths	
	grass
Voles	
Weasels	mice, voles
Tree-living insects	trees
	tree-living insects, mites
Fungi	trees
Mites	
	ground-living insects
Owls	

3

DO NOT WRITE IN THIS MARGIN

Marks | KU | PS

1. (*a*) (continued)

(ii) Use the food web to complete the food chain below, consisting of four organisms.

ferns → moths → mice → weasels **1** | 1

(*b*) Trees are producers and mice are consumers.

What is the meaning of the terms producer and consumer?

Producer makes it's own food using sun energy **1** | 1

Consumer relys on other animals / plants for food **1** | 1

[Turn over

Marks | KU | PS

2. Some features of six species of the buttercup family are shown in the table below.

Species name	Leaves	Runners	Stem
Greater spearwort	toothed	present	hairy
Meadow buttercup	lobed	absent	hairy
Lesser celandine	heart-shaped	absent	hairless
Creeping buttercup	lobed	present	hairy
Lesser spearwort	toothed	absent	hairless
Celery-leaved buttercup	lobed	absent	hairless

(a) Use the information in the table to complete the key below.
Write the correct feature on each dotted line and the correct names in the empty boxes.

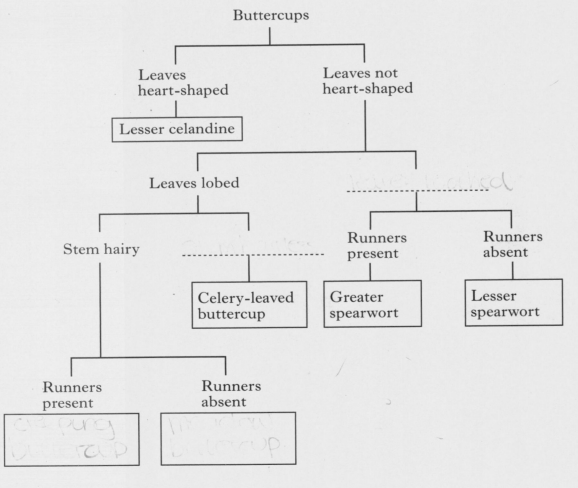

3

DO NOT
WRITE IN
THIS
MARGIN

2. (continued)

(b) Which feature could be used to distinguish between a Lesser celandine and a Lesser spearwort?

leaus heart-shaped

Marks **1**   KU   PS **1**

(c) Which features do the Meadow buttercup and the Celery-leaved buttercup have in common?

runners absent

Marks **1**   KU   PS **0**

[Turn over

3. (a) A population survey of barnacles and mussels between the high and low tide marks of a rocky shore was carried out using quadrats.

The results are shown in the table below.

Tide mark	High								➤ Low	
Quadrat number	1	2	3	4	5	6	7	8	9	10
Number of mussels	0	2	15	31	32	34	50	55	58	60
Number of barnacles	52	51	37	40	40	23	15	17	15	10

(i) On the grid below, complete the bar chart by

    1. adding a scale to the vertical axis

    2. plotting the bars for the barnacles in quadrats 5–10

(An additional grid, if needed, will be found on page 27.)

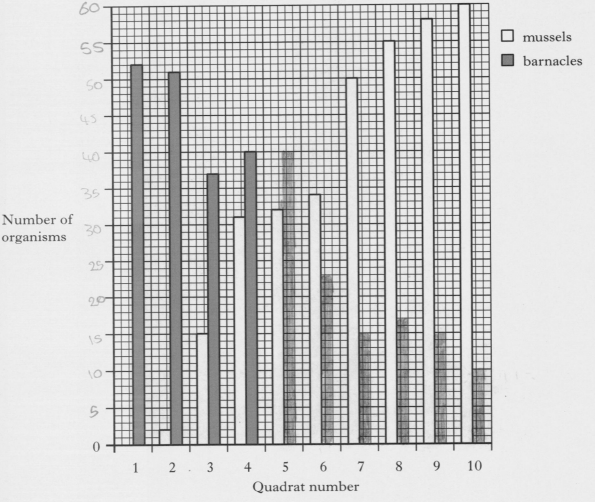

Marks | KU | PS

3. (*a*) (continued)

(ii) Calculate the average number of barnacles per quadrat.

Space for calculation

Average number _____ 3   **1**   0

(iii) What is the trend shown by the number of mussels from the high to the low tide marks?

it increases as you get closer to low tide mark   **1**   1

(*b*) The mussels and the barnacles are in competition with each other.

State **one** possible effect on the mussel population of **reduced competition** from barnacles.

~~there~~ the number of mussels will increase   **1**   1

(*c*) The following factors affect populations of barnacles and mussels.

Underline **two** abiotic factors from the list.

List of factors   water temperature
disease
predators
salt concentration
food supply   **1**   1

(*d*) A rocky shore ecosystem consists of a community of organisms and one other part.

Name the other part.

habitat   **1**   1

[**Turn over**

4. (*a*) In an investigation on photosynthesis, two bell jars were set up as shown below and left in bright light.

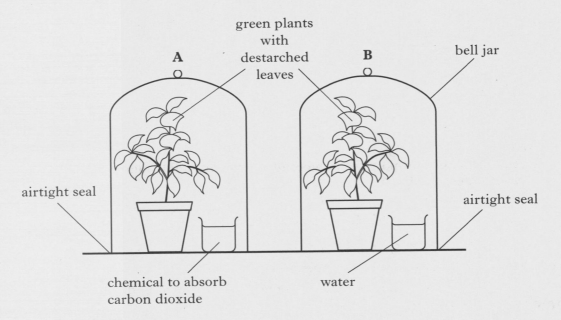

green plants with destarched leaves

A   B   bell jar

airtight seal   airtight seal

chemical to absorb carbon dioxide   water

After 48 hours a leaf was removed from each plant and tested for starch.

(i) In which plant would photosynthesis take place? Give a reason for your answer.

Plant _____A_____

Reason _____

_____ **1**

(ii) Name a product of photosynthesis, other than carbohydrate.

_____Oxygen_____ **1**

(iii) Why were the plants destarched before being used in the investigation?

So that the experiment can take place fairly. **1**

(iv) Give **one** feature of the plants that would have to be kept the same to allow a fair comparison in the investigation.

the time the plants were left in the bell jars. **1**

Marks | KU | PS

4. **(continued)**

(b) Name the structures in a leaf through which gases can pass.

Stems

1

(c) Name the chemical found in leaves that converts light energy into chemical energy during photosynthesis.

1

(d) The grid below refers to parts of a flower.

A sepal	B petal	C stamen	D anther
E stigma	F ovary	G nectary	H ovule

Use letters from the grid to answer the following questions.

(i) Which structure protects the flower bud?

A

1

(ii) Which structure receives pollen grains?

G

1

(iii) Which structure develops into a fruit after fertilisation?

H

1

[Turn over

5. (a) The diagram represents the reproductive system of a human female.

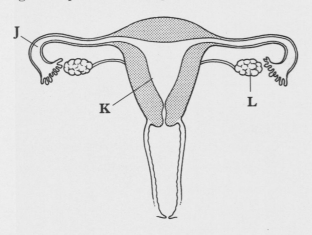

(i) Name the parts labelled on the diagram.

J ____~~ette~~ oviduct____

K ____womb____

L ____ovaries____

(ii) In the table below, match each letter from the diagram to its correct function.

Function	Letter
Eggs produced	L
Fertilisation takes place	K
Fertilised egg becomes attached	J

(b) Tick (✓) boxes in the table to indicate whether each of the following statements is true for eggs, sperm, or both.

Statement	Eggs	Sperm
Contain a food store for developing fetus	✓	
Swim using a tail		✓
Produced in testes		✓
In most fish, are deposited into the water	✓	
Are gametes	✓	✓

Marks: 2 (KU 2)

Marks: 2 (KU 1)

Marks: 2 (KU 1)

6. The apparatus shown was set up to investigate the behaviour of woodlice.

At the start of the investigation 20 woodlice were placed in the centre of the chamber. After 10 minutes there were 2 on side A and 18 on side B.

(a) What environmental factor was being investigated?

moisture

Marks **1**

(b) Describe the response of the woodlice in the investigation.

they were attracted to the side with water

1

(c) Why were the woodlice left for ten minutes before the results were taken?

to give them time to respond to the new environment.

1

(d) Why were 20 woodlice used, rather than one?

to make the results more reliable.

1

(e) Name **one** abiotic factor which should be kept constant during the investigation.

light

1

(f) Suggest **two** changes which could be made to the apparatus in order to investigate the response of woodlice to light.

1 _put a dark piece of paper over one side_

1

2 _leave the other side open to allow sunlight in_

1

Marks | KU | PS

7. (a) Complete the table by using all the letters from the list to identify the parts found in each type of cell.

Each part may be used **once** or **more than once**.

Parts of cells

A   cell membrane
B   cell wall
C   chloroplast
D   cytoplasm
E   nucleus

Leaf cell	Cheek cell
A B C	B E D

2

(b) Use the information in the table below to answer the questions about liquids used in preparing microscope slides.

Type of cell	Liquid used	Effect
human cheek cell	methylene blue	nucleus turns blue
onion epidermal cell	iodine solution	nucleus turns yellow
human skin cell	eosin	cytoplasm turns pink
onion root cell	acetic orcein	chromosomes turn red

(i) Name **two** liquids used to prepare plant cells.

1   acetic orcein

2   iodine solution

1

(ii) What effect does eosin have on skin cells?

cytoplasm turns pink

1

(iii) Which liquid could be used to show stages of mitosis?

methylene blue

1

Marks | KU | PS

7. (continued)

(c) What name is given to a liquid that is used to make the parts of a cell clearer when viewed under a microscope?

Iodine solution

1

(d) The magnification of a microscope is calculated using the following formula.

**Total magnification = eyepiece lens × objective lens
                          magnification   magnification**

Use the formula to complete the following table.

The same eyepiece was used each time.

Power	Eyepiece lens magnification	Objective lens magnification	Total magnification
Low	× 12	× 4	48
Medium	×12	× 10	×120
High	× 12	×40	× 480

2

[Turn over

8. (a) The statements in the table describe the movement of substances into or out of cells.

Number	Statement
1	glucose moves from the small intestine into the blood
2	water enters root cells from the soil
3	carbon dioxide passes from the blood into the lungs

(i) Which statement is an example of osmosis?

Statement number ___2___

1

(ii) What term could be used to describe the movement of substances in all of the examples?

___difusion___

1

(b) Pieces of potato were weighed, placed in sugar solutions of different concentrations for one hour, then reweighed.

The graph below shows the percentage change in mass at each concentration.

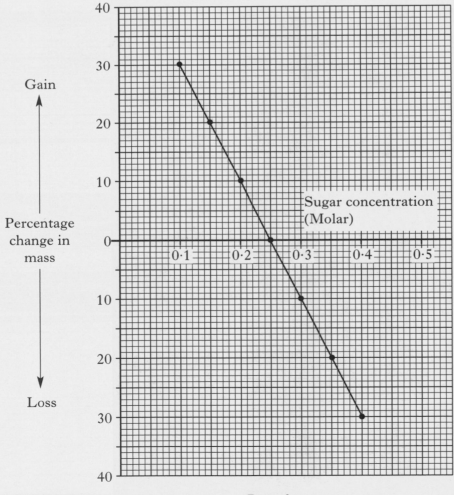

8. (b) (continued)

(i) The movement of what substance is responsible for the change in mass?

_____sugar_____

Marks **1**

(ii) What was the percentage change in mass of the piece of potato placed in the 0·15 Molar solution?

____30____ %

1

(iii) What was the concentration of the solution which caused the potato to lose 30% of its original mass?

_____ Molar

1

(iv) At what concentration was there no change in mass of the potato?

_____ Molar

1

[Turn over

9. Read the following passage carefully.

Adapted from *"Stirring Stuff's in the bag"*, The Herald, April 2002.

Pausing for a cup of tea is a good way to take time out in a busy day. About 135 million cups are consumed in Britain daily.

Favourite "cuppas" include first thing in the morning before getting ready for work, during a busy day and at the end of the day to relax. Relaxation is the most common mood when taking a tea break.

As well as relieving stress, tea can also be a life-saver. Research has shown that the great British "cuppa" has disease-fighting capabilities. A cup of tea can have protective effects against cancer and heart disease. A mixture of green tea and black tea rubbed on cancerous areas reduced cell growth. Tests show that tea slows the development of lung cancers and some bowel cancers. It is also thought to decrease the risk of cancer of the digestive system. Red tea from South Africa is rich in antioxidants and free from tannin and caffeine which are found in many other teas.

The three basic types of tea, black, green and oolong, give rise to more than 3000 varieties, each having its own distinct character. People are now trying different styles of teas such as organic, Chai spice, decaffeinated, herbal and iced tea.

Answer the following questions, based on the above passage.

(a) How much tea is drunk in Britain daily?

about 135 million

1

(b) What is the most common mood whilst drinking tea?

Relaxation

1

(c) Apart from cancer, what disease can tea help prevent?

heart disease

1

(d) Name **three** types of cancer that tea may help prevent.

1 _lung_ 2 _bowel_ 3 _digestive system_

1

(e) What **two** substances are not present in South African red tea?

tannin & caffine

1

(f) Name **three** styles of tea, mentioned in the passage, that people are now trying.

1 _organic_ 2 _chai spice_ 3 _herbal_

1

10. The bar graph shows the body lengths in a population of 300 budgerigars.
The pie chart shows the colours in the same population.

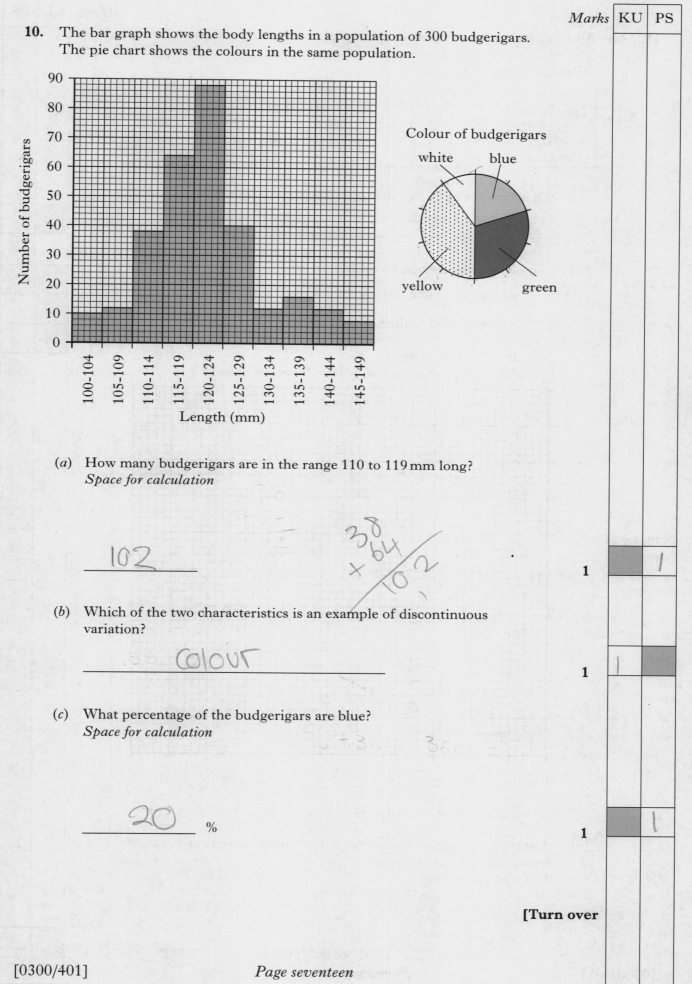

(a) How many budgerigars are in the range 110 to 119 mm long?
Space for calculation

_____102_____

38
+ 64
/ 10 2

1   1

(b) Which of the two characteristics is an example of discontinuous
variation?

_____colour_____

1   1

(c) What percentage of the budgerigars are blue?
Space for calculation

_____20_____ %

1   1

[Turn over

Marks | KU | PS

11. (*a*) An investigation was carried out into the growth of a bacterial culture. The numbers of bacteria were counted every 30 minutes and the results are shown in the table below.

Time (minutes)	0	30	60	90	120	150
Number of bacteria (thousands per mm^3)	3	6	12	24	48	96

(i) What happens to the number of bacteria every 30 minutes?

it doubles

1

(ii) Complete the line graph below by

1   adding a suitable scale to the y-axis

1

2   adding a label to the x-axis

1

3   plotting the graph.

1

(An additional grid, if needed, will be found on page 28.)

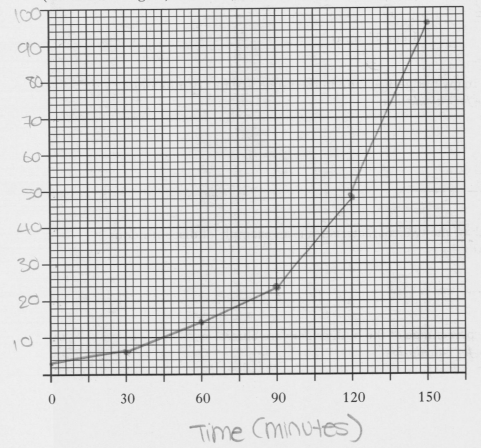

Number of bacteria (thousands per mm^3)

Time (minutes)

(iii) Assuming no change in conditions, how many bacteria cells would be present after 240 minutes?
Space for calculation

180   192
210   384
240   768

768 _____ thousands per mm^3

1

Marks | KU | PS

11. **(continued)**

(b) The following diagrams show four stages of mitotic cell division but not in the correct order.

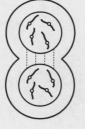   

A   B   C   D

Arrange the letters from the diagrams to put the stages into the correct order. The first stage has been given.

1st stage _____C_____

2nd stage _____B_____

3rd stage _____B A_____

4th stage _____A D_____

1

(c) Complete the following sentence by underlining the correct option in each group.

In comparison with the original cell, the number of chromosomes present in a cell produced by mitosis is { greater / smaller / the same } and it contains { different / the same } information.

1

[Turn over

12. (a) The diagram shows some of the structures of the human eye.

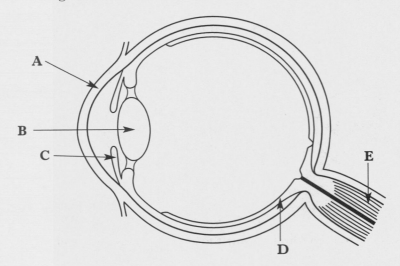

Complete the table to show the names and functions of the structures labelled.

Letter	Name of structure	Function
A	lense	Allows light to enter the eye
B		allows you to see
C	Iris	Protects the eye
D	P...	Converts light into electrical impulses
E	Optic nerve	allows you to move eye

3

(b) Humans have two eyes and two ears. What does this contribute to their sight and hearing?

Sight _unproves the sight as you have two eyes instead of one_

1

Hearing _allows you to hear sound in different directions_

1

DO NOT
WRITE IN
THIS
MARGIN

Marks | KU | PS

12. **(continued)**

(c) The diagram represents the flow of information in the human nervous system.

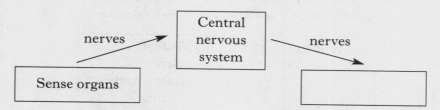

(i) Complete the diagram by writing the missing word in the box.   **1**

(ii) Name the two main parts of the central nervous system.

1 _____ 2 _____   **1**

[Turn over

13. (*a*) The table gives information about components of the blood.
Use the information provided to answer the questions which follow.

Appearance under a microscope (not drawn to the same scale)	Number per mm³ of blood	Diameter in millimetres	Additional information
Red blood cells	5·5 million	0·008	Made in marrow of bones. Iron essential. 2 million made each second. Last for about 4 months.
White blood cells	8000	0·02	Made in marrow of bones or in lymph nodes. Fight infection by engulfing bacteria or producing antibodies.
Platelets	400,000	0·003	Made in marrow. Contain proteins which form blood clots.

(i) Name **two** places where blood cells are made.

1 marrow of bones   2 lymph nodes

1

(ii) Which cells are the largest?

white red blood cells

1

(iii) Which component is present in the greatest numbers?

Red blood cells

1

(iv) What type of substance is needed to form blood clots?

platelets

1

13. **(a)** **(continued)**

(v) Describe **two** ways in which white blood cells fight infection.

1 _engulfing bacteria_

2 _producing antibodies_

(vi) On average, how many red blood cells are made in an hour?
Space for calculation

_120, ~~00000~~_ million

(b) The diagram below represents the site of gas exchange between a blood vessel and the muscle cells of a mammal.

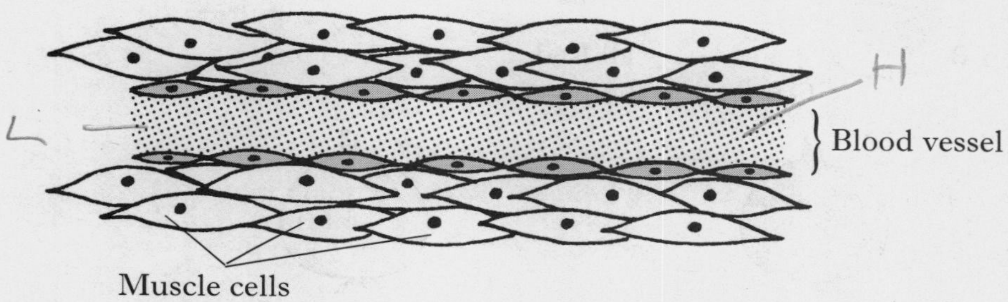

Muscle cells

(i) Name the type of blood vessel shown.

capillaries

(ii) On the diagram, write the letter **H** to indicate an area where the oxygen concentration is relatively high and the letter **L** to indicate where it is relatively low.

(c) In which component of blood is most of the oxygen carried?

Red blood ~~cells~~ vessels

[Turn over

DO NOT WRITE IN THIS MARGIN

Marks	KU	PS

14. (*a*) A mule is produced by mating a horse and a donkey.
Mules are always infertile. What information does this provide about horses and donkeys?

They are able to infertile mules. **1**

(*b*) The diagram below shows inheritance of colour in onions.

×

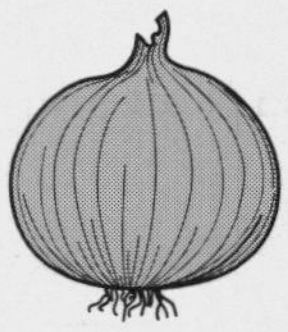

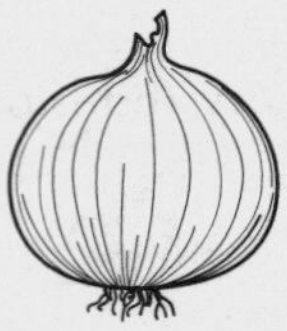

Generation A — Red — White

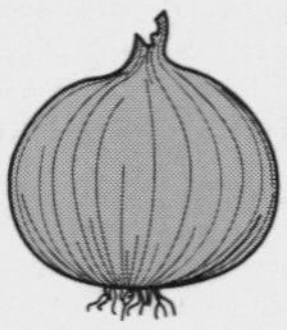

Generation B — all Red

Generation B onions self-crossed

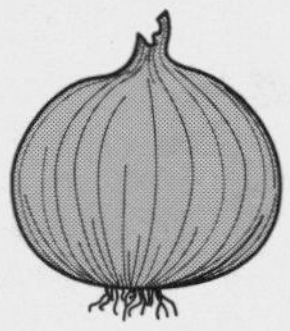

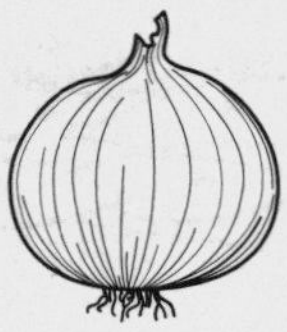

Generation C — 36 Red — 9 White

(i) Which onion colour is dominant?

Red **1**

(ii) Complete the table with the correct symbols to identify each of the generations shown in the diagram.

Generation	*Symbol*
A	**P**
B	f1
C	f2

1

(iii) Calculate the simple whole number ratio of red onions to white onions produced in Generation C.

Space for calculation

36 : 9
12 : 3
4 : 1

4 : 1
Red onions : White onions **1**

DO NOT WRITE IN THIS MARGIN

Marks | KU | PS

15. Thalassaemia is an inherited disease which prevents people producing blood cells. The family tree shows inheritance of thalassaemia.

☐ Unaffected male   ■ Thalassaemic male

◯ Unaffected female   ● Thalassaemic female

(a)   (i)   Which of the following statements about Parents A and B is true?
Tick (✓) the correct box.

Both have the thalassaemic gene.   ☐

One has the thalassaemic gene.   ☐

Neither has the thalassaemic gene.   ☑   1

(ii)   Give a reason for your answer.

_____   1

(b)   What proportion of the children of Parents A and B were thalassaemic?

_____ 2/4 _____ ½ _____   1

(c)   Doctors can test for thalassaemia by examining the cells of a fetus. The cells are obtained by inserting a needle into the mother's uterus and withdrawing fluid from around the fetus.

What name is given to this procedure?

_____   1

[Turn over

Marks | KU | PS

16. Yeast is a micro-organism which carries out fermentation.

(a) Complete the following word equation for fermentation in yeast.

| glucose | → | alcohol ~~energy~~ | + | oxygen | + | **energy** |

1

(b) Name **two** manufacturing processes which depend on fermentation by yeast.

1 Brewing

2 Baking

1

(c) Complete the following sentence by underlining the correct word in each group.

Yeast is a { fungus / bacterium } and is { single- / multi- } celled.

1

(d) Describe the precautions which should be taken with each of the following items when working with micro-organisms.

1 Bench surfaces sterised to kill bacteria

1

2 Wire loops for inoculating a plate held over the flame to kill bacteria

1

(e) Petri dishes half-filled with agar gel are used to grow micro-organisms.

Explain why Petri dishes containing micro-organisms must be kept closed.

to stop unwanted micro-organism getting in.

1

[END OF QUESTION PAPER]

SPACE FOR ANSWERS
AND FOR ROUGH WORKING

ADDITIONAL GRID FOR QUESTION 3(*a*)(i)

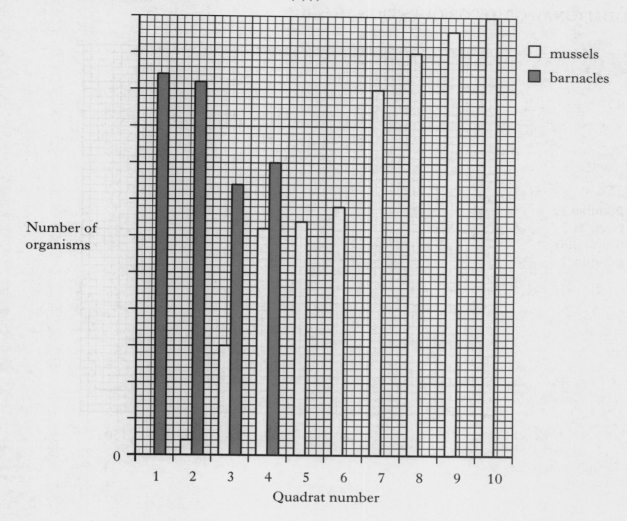

SPACE FOR ANSWERS
AND FOR ROUGH WORKING

ADDITIONAL GRID FOR QUESTION 11(*a*)(ii)

Number of
bacteria
(thousands
per mm³)

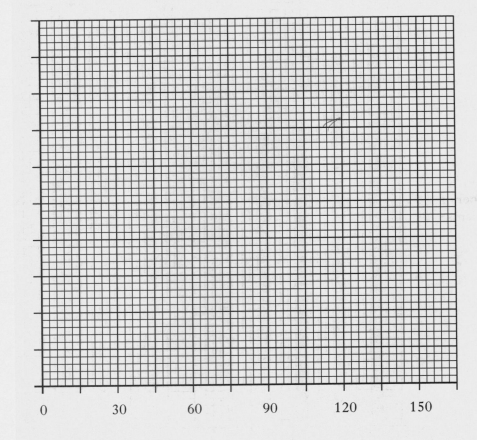

[BLANK PAGE]

G

FOR OFFICIAL USE

KU   PS

Total Marks

0300/401

NATIONAL
QUALIFICATIONS
2005

WEDNESDAY, 18 MAY
9.00 AM – 10.30 AM

BIOLOGY
STANDARD GRADE
General Level

Fill in these boxes and read what is printed below.

Full name of centre

Town

Forename(s)

Surname

Date of birth
Day Month Year   Scottish candidate number   Number of seat

1 All questions should be attempted.

2 The questions may be answered in any order but all answers are to be written in the spaces provided in this answer book, and must be written clearly and legibly in ink.

3 Rough work, if any should be necessary, as well as the fair copy, is to be written in this book. Additional spaces for answers and for rough work will be found at the end of the book. Rough work should be scored through when the fair copy has been written.

4 Before leaving the examination room you must give this book to the invigilator. If you do not, you may lose all the marks for this paper.

SCOTTISH
QUALIFICATIONS
AUTHORITY

©

1. Part of a woodland food web is shown below.

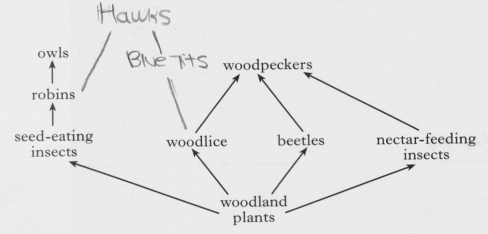

(a) (i) What do the arrows in the food web represent?

the energy flow

1

(ii) How many food chains in the food web involve woodpeckers?

three

1

(iii) Blue tits eat woodlice. Hawks eat blue tits and robins.

Add blue tits and hawks to the food web diagram to show their feeding relationships.

1

(b) A study of the populations of beetles and woodlice in an area of woodland was carried out over a number of years.

The results are shown below.

Year of study	Number of beetles	Number of woodlice
1	563	540
2	641	672
3	682	698
4	117	940

(i) Use information from **both** the table **and** the food web to suggest an explanation for the drop in the number of beetles in year 4 of the study.

woodpeckers eat both woodlice &
beetles so if there is an increase
in woodlice the woodpeckers are
obviously eating more beetles.

1

1.(b) (continued)

(ii) During the same period, the numbers of owls increased.

Explain this change in terms of their birth rate and death rate.

The cubs ith yo   and

death rate ncreased.

1

(iii) What change in the population of the robins could have caused the increase in the number of owls?

_.._

1

(c) When a plant or animal dies, decay takes place.

Choose words from the box below to complete the following sentences about decay.

You may use each word **once**, **more than once** or **not at all**.

soil	animals	nutrients
plants	protein	micro-organisms

Decay is carried out by _Micro organisms_ .

This process releases _____ which can be absorbed

by _soil_ .

2

[Turn over

Marks | KU | PS

2. (a) The following table gives the results of an investigation on the factors affecting seed germination.

Test tube	Conditions provided		
	Temperature (°C)	Water present	Oxygen present
1	20	yes	yes
2	20	yes	no
3	20	no	yes
4	0	yes	yes
5	0	no	yes

In which tube(s) would germination occur?

_____

1

(b) The diagram shows a section through a seed.

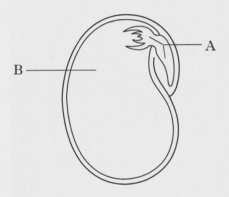

(i) Name the parts labelled A and B.

A _____Roots_____

1

B _____

1

(ii) Name the part of a seed which protects the internal structures.

_____

1

Marks | KU | PS

2. (continued)

(c) The table below shows the time from germination to flowering for some plant species.

Plant species	Time from germination to flowering (years)
Rock rose	2·0
Hollyhock	0·5
Broom	3·0
Birch	10·0
Phlox	1·0
Berberis	5·5

Use the information from the table to complete the **bar chart** below by:

(i) labelling the vertical axis;   1

(ii) adding an appropriate scale to the vertical axis;   1

(iii) drawing the bars.   1

(Additional graph paper, if required, will be found on page 30.)

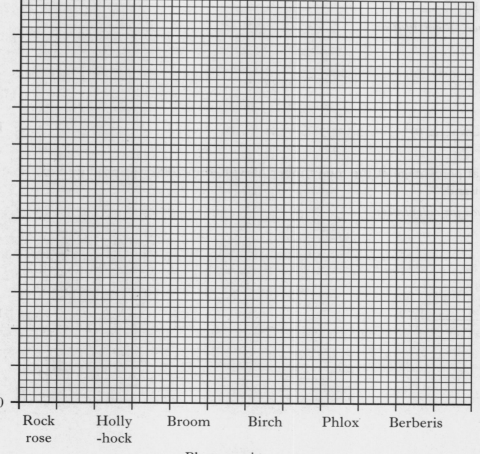

Plant species

[Turn over

3. The table below gives information about the harvest of softwood timber over a 3 year period.

Country	Timber harvested each year (m³)		
	1999	2000	2001
Scotland	2292	2496	2883
England	699	881	913
Wales	385	463	663
Total	3376	3840	

(a) Complete the table to show the totals harvested in 1999 and in 2001.

Space for calculations

1

(b) What was the increase in timber harvested in Wales between 1999 and 2001?

Space for calculation

_____ m³

1

(c) What percentage of the total timber harvested in 2000 was produced in Scotland?

Space for calculation

_____%

1

DO NOT
WRITE IN
THIS
MARGIN

	Marks	KU	PS

4. The following sentences refer to food manufacture and transport in plants. Underline **one** alternative in each bracket to make the sentences correct.

(a) Light energy is converted to chemical energy by $\left\{ \begin{array}{c} \text{carbon dioxide} \\ \text{chlorophyll} \end{array} \right\}$.   **1**

(b) Food is transported from the leaves in $\left\{ \begin{array}{c} \text{xylem} \\ \text{phloem} \end{array} \right\}$.   **1**

(c) The raw materials for photosynthesis are $\left\{ \begin{array}{c} \text{carbon dioxide} \\ \text{oxygen} \end{array} \right\}$ and $\left\{ \begin{array}{c} \text{glucose} \\ \text{water} \end{array} \right\}$.   **1**

(d) Food may be stored in the leaves as $\left\{ \begin{array}{c} \text{glucose} \\ \text{starch} \end{array} \right\}$.   **1**

[Turn over

5. The diagram shows a choice chamber which could be used to investigate the behaviour of woodlice.

woodlice

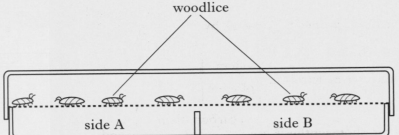

side A   side B

(a) How could the choice chamber be set up to study the effect of light on the behaviour of woodlice?

in one side

1

(b) (i) Name **one** other abiotic factor which may affect woodlice behaviour that can be investigated using a choice chamber.

Moisture

1

(ii) How could the choice chamber be set up to investigate this other abiotic factor?

put water in one side

1

DO NOT WRITE IN THIS MARGIN

Marks | KU | PS

6. The effect of practice on the reaction times of three volunteers was investigated. A buzzer was sounded and the time taken to stop a clock was measured.

Each volunteer was tested 10 times.

The results are shown in the table.

Volunteer \ *Attempt*	*Reaction time (milliseconds)* 1	2	3	4	5	6	7	8	9	10
A	256	250	210	207	201	192	187	164	162	154
B	234	227	218	201	200	185	179	161	153	147
C	218	200	195	192	186	178	160	149	136	131

(*a*) Why were three volunteers tested rather than one?

Reliable results

1

(*b*) The average reaction time of the three volunteers' first attempts was 236 milliseconds.

Calculate the average reaction time of their final attempts.

Space for calculation

144 milliseconds

1

(*c*) From the results of the investigation, describe the effect of practice on reaction time.

The more they practised the [illegible]

they [illegible]

1

[Turn over

Marks | KU | PS

7. (a) The following list contains descriptions of stages in the reproduction of a mammal.

   A   A sperm nucleus joins with an egg nucleus.
   B   The embryo develops in the amniotic sac.
   C   The embryo becomes attached to the uterus wall.
   D   A fertilised egg passes down the oviduct.
   E   The young animal is born.

   Arrange the stages into the correct order by writing the letters into the boxes.

$$A \rightarrow \boxed{} \rightarrow \boxed{} \rightarrow \boxed{} \rightarrow E$$

1

   (b) The diagrams show the human female and male reproductive systems.

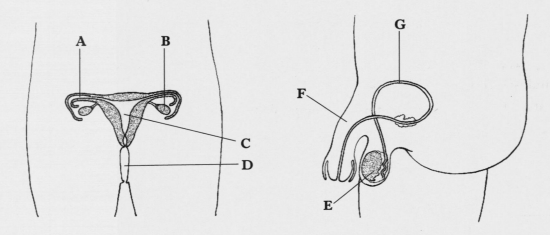

   Complete the table below by adding the correct letter, name and function of the parts.

Letter	Name	Function
C	ovary	
		where the embryo develops
E		

3

DO NOT WRITE IN THIS MARGIN

	Marks	KU	PS

7. (continued)

(*c*) (i) Mammal embryos obtain their food from their mother's blood.

Where do the embryos of fish obtain their food?

____ **1**

(ii) Young fish care for themselves.

How are young mammals cared for?

____ **1**

[Turn over

Marks | KU | PS

8. (a) The diagram represents a section through the heart of a mammal.

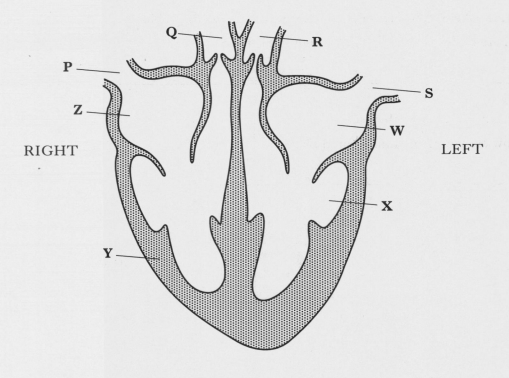

RIGHT   LEFT

Use letters from the diagram to identify the following.

(i) The two atria (auricles).

_____ and _____

1

(ii) The vessel which brings blood to the heart from the lungs.

_____

1

(iii) The two vessels which carry deoxygenated blood.

_____ and _____

1

(b) Explain why the wall of the left ventricle is thicker than the wall of the right ventricle.

_____

_____

1

DO NOT WRITE IN THIS MARGIN

Marks | KU | PS

8. (continued)

(*c*) (i) Use lines to connect each of the blood vessels to the correct description of blood flow.

Blood vessel	*Description of blood flow*
arteries	away from the heart
veins	through the tissues
capillaries	towards the heart

2

(ii) In which type of blood vessel may a pulse be felt?

____

1

[Turn over

Marks | KU | PS

9. The pulse rate of an athlete was monitored during a training exercise. The results are shown in the table.

Time (minutes)	0	1	2	3	4	5	6	7	8
Pulse rate (beats per minute)	65	65	90	118	118	118	105	100	80

(a) Complete the line graph of the results by

   (i)   labelling and adding an appropriate scale to the horizontal axis, **1**

   (ii) plotting the graph. **1**

   The first three points have been plotted.

   (Additional graph paper, if required, will be found on page 31.)

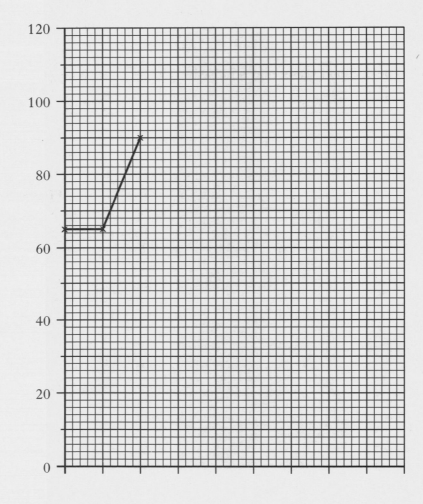

Pulse rate (beats per minute)

(b) What evidence suggests that the athlete had not fully recovered at 8 minutes? **1**

DO NOT WRITE IN THIS MARGIN

Marks KU PS

9. **(continued)**

(*c*) **Suggest an improvement to the procedure to allow the recovery time of the athlete to be measured.**

____

____ **1**

(*d*) **How might the recovery time of the athlete differ from that of an untrained person?**

____

____ **1**

[Turn over

10. Read the following passage and answer the questions based on it.

Hayfever

Hayfever affects 2 to 3 million people in Britain. It is caused by an allergy to pollen or sometimes the spores of fungi. The body's immune system reacts by releasing excess histamine. This results in an irritation and inflammation of the nose and eyes.

The symptoms vary and may involve sneezing, a runny or blocked nose, and a sore throat. The eyes may become red, watery or itchy. In addition, a wheezy chest may suggest that the sufferer also has asthma. The peak pollen time is early summer when school and university examinations take place. This can make it difficult to revise and perform well.

Hayfever is related to asthma and eczema. It is quite common to find members of the same family with one or more of these conditions.

Various treatments are available without prescription. These include antihistamine tablets to reduce the allergic response as well as nasal sprays and eye drops to reduce inflammation. For severe cases, doctors may prescribe either tablets or injections containing steroids. These can cause side effects so the benefits have to be weighed against the possible disadvantages. Tablets are more favoured than injections. Other types of injection can desensitise patients to the pollen causing their allergy. Unfortunately, they may produce serious side effects and, as they can only be given under close hospital supervision, are hardly ever used.

(a) What effect does pollen have on the body's immune system in hayfever sufferers?

_____ 1

(b) What evidence is there that hayfever might have a genetic component?

_____ 1

(c) Which symptom suggests that a hayfever sufferer may also have asthma?

_____ 1

DO NOT WRITE IN THIS MARGIN

Marks	KU	PS

10. (continued)

(*d*) At what time of the year are hayfever sufferers likely to be worst affected? **1**

____

(*e*) What type of substance is found in treatments prescribed for severe cases of hayfever? **1**

____

(*f*) Why are desensitising injections not used very often? **1**

____

[Turn over

Marks | KU | PS

11. (*a*) The bar chart shows the results of a survey into blood groups of a sample of people in a Scottish town (Town X).

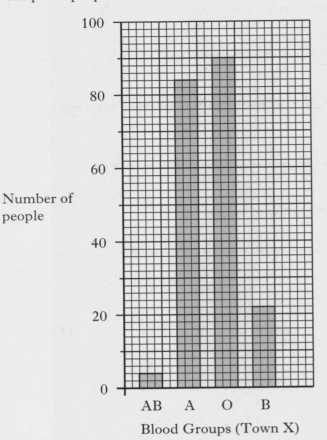

Number of people

Blood Groups (Town X)

(i) Is the variation in blood group continuous or discontinuous?

_____

1

(ii) How many people were in the survey?
Space for calculation

Number of people _____

1

Marks | KU | PS

11. **(continued)**

(b) A similar survey was carried out on a sample of 1000 people in a different town of the same size (Town Y).

There were 20 with group AB, 500 with group A, 400 with group O and 80 with group B.

(i) Complete the pie chart of these results by drawing and labelling the remaining segments.

(An additional chart, if required, will be found on page 31.)

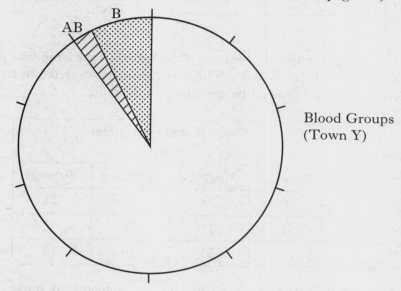

Blood Groups
(Town Y)

2

(ii) What percentage of people in the Town Y sample had blood group O?

Space for calculation

_____ %

1

(c) (i) Select **one** similarity and **one** difference between the results of the surveys for Towns X and Y.

Similarity _____

1

Difference _____

1

(ii) Which blood group survey, Town X or Town Y, is the more reliable?

Give a reason for your answer.

Town _____

1

Reason _____

1

Page nineteen

[Turn over

Marks | KU | PS

12. Maggots move away from light. The effect of different light intensities on the rate of movement was investigated using the apparatus shown below.

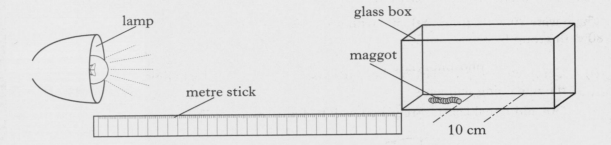

The time taken for a maggot to move 10 cm was recorded when the lamp was at different distances from the glass box. The experiment was carried out using three different maggots. The results are shown in the table.

Distance between lamp and box (cm)	Time taken to move 10 cm (seconds)			
	Maggot 1	Maggot 2	Maggot 3	Average
100	30	33	30	31
50	23	24	22	
25	18	20	19	19

(a) Complete the table with the average time for the maggots to move 10 cm when the lamp was at a distance of 50 cm.

Space for calculation

1

(b) Underline **one** option in each bracket to complete the following sentences correctly.

As the distance between the lamp and the glass box decreases, the light

intensity $\left\{ \begin{array}{l} \text{increases} \\ \text{decreases} \\ \text{stays the same} \end{array} \right\}$.

1

As the light intensity decreases, the time taken for the maggot to move

10 cm $\left\{ \begin{array}{l} \text{increases} \\ \text{decreases} \\ \text{stays the same} \end{array} \right\}$.

1

(c) What would happen to the rate of movement of the maggots if they were placed in darkness?

_____

1

13. Phosphorylase is an enzyme extracted from potatoes. Drops of phosphorylase, glucose-1-phosphate and water were added to a dimple tile as shown.

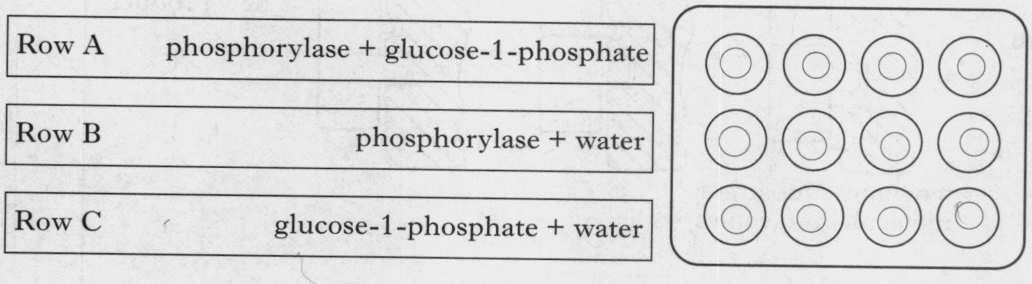

Row A	phosphorylase + glucose-1-phosphate
Row B	phosphorylase + water
Row C	glucose-1-phosphate + water

A drop of iodine solution was added to one dimple in each row at three-minute intervals. If starch is present, a black colour forms.

The results are shown below.

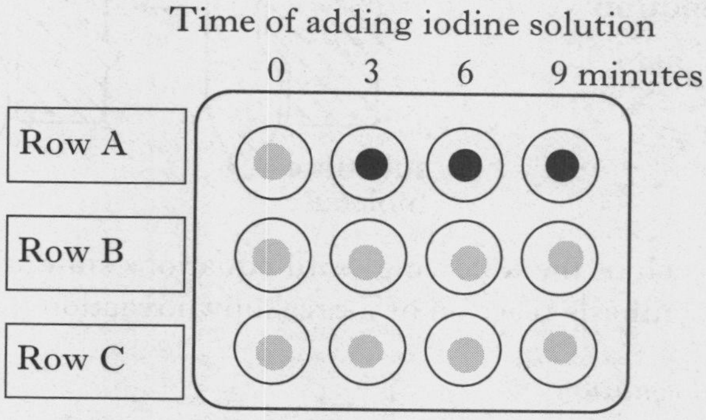

Time of adding iodine solution

0   3   6   9 minutes

Row A

Row B

Row C

(a) In which row has starch been synthesised?

Row _____

1

(b) The experiment was carried out at 25 °C. How would the results in Row A differ if the experiment had been carried out at a lower temperature?

_____

1

(c) Rows B and C are control experiments.

(i) What conclusion can be drawn from Row B?_____

_____

1

(ii) What conclusion can be drawn from Row C?_____

_____

1

[Turn over

Official SQA Past Papers: General Biology 2005

DO NOT
WRITE IN
THIS
MARGIN

Marks | KU | PS

14. The diagrams show two different types of enzyme-controlled reactions.

Diagram 1
Synthesis reaction

enzyme   substrate
molecule   molecules

new product

Diagram 2
Breakdown reaction

enzyme
molecule

2 new
products
formed

substrate
molecule

(a) For each of the following word equations state whether it is an example of a synthesis reaction or a breakdown reaction.

Word equation   *Type of reaction*

(i) maltose $\xrightarrow{\text{enzyme X}}$ glucose molecules _____

(ii) amino acid molecules $\xrightarrow{\text{enzyme Y}}$ protein molecule _____

(iii) fatty acids and glycerol $\xrightarrow{\text{enzyme Z}}$ fat molecule _____ **2**

(b) Of what type of substance are enzymes made?

_____

1

(c) Respiration provides energy for cells to carry out various functions.

Underline **two** of the following functions which require energy from respiration.

Muscle contraction   Osmosis   Diffusion   Cell division   **1**

Marks | KU | PS

15. (a) The following grid contains some terms used in studying inheritance.

A gamete formation	B tallness in peas	C genotype
D phenotype	E true breeding	F gene
G fertilisation	H dominant	I dwarfness in peas

Use letters from the grid to identify the correct term for each of the following.

(i) Part of a chromosome _____ 1

(ii) Involves a reduction in the number of chromosomes _____ 1

(iii) Two different phenotypes of the same characteristic _____

and _____ 1

(iv) An organism with only one form of a particular gene _____ 1

(v) The genes that an organism contains for a characteristic _____ 1

(b) Pea plant cells contain 14 chromosomes.

(i) How many complete sets of chromosomes does this represent?

_____ sets 1

(ii) How many chromosomes are there in the sex cells of pea plants?
Space for calculation

_____ chromosomes 1

[Turn over

16. The diagram shows the apparatus used to produce large numbers of bacterial cells for manufacturing insulin.

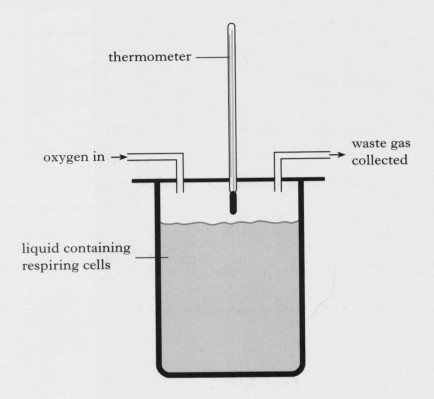

thermometer —

oxygen in →

waste gas collected

liquid containing respiring cells

(a) Suggest an improvement which could be made to the way the apparatus is set up and explain why it is necessary.

Improvement _____   1

Explanation _____

_____   1

(b) (i) Which type of respiration will take place because of the presence of oxygen?

_____   1

(ii) What additional factor, not shown in the diagram, must be supplied to allow the bacteria to respire?

_____   1

DO NOT
WRITE IN
THIS
MARGIN

	Marks	KU	PS

16. **(b)** **(continued)**

(iii) What waste gas will be produced during respiration?

_____ **1**

(iv) What form of energy, other than chemical, may be released by the bacterial cells during respiration?

_____ **1**

[Turn over

DO NOT
WRITE IN
THIS
MARGIN

Marks | KU | PS

17. A sewage works removes organic material before water is discharged into a river. This is done in two main stages.

Stage 1 Organic solids settle out as sludge which is treated separately.

Stage 2 The remaining liquid is treated with living organisms.

(a) (i) Name **one** useful product which can be made from the treated sludge produced in Stage 1.

_____

1

(ii) What type of organisms act on the liquid in Stage 2?

_____

1

(iii) Describe **one** way in which oxygen can be provided for the organisms in Stage 2.

_____

_____

1

17. (continued)

(b) When water from a sewage works is analysed, several measurements are made. The table shows some of the measurements taken over one year.

Month	Suspended solids (mg/l)	Biochemical oxygen demand (mg/l)
January	35·0	31·0
February	42·0	40·0
March	44·0	35·5
April	30·5	18·0
May	27·0	17·0
June	29·5	19·0
July	21·5	14·5
August	25·5	16·5
September	25·5	16·5
October	29·5	22·0
November	34·5	28·5
December	32·5	35·0

(i) Sewage works should not discharge water with more than 30 mg/l suspended solids **and** a biochemical oxygen demand of more than 20 mg/l.

In which months of the year was water from the sewage works not meeting this standard?

_____

_____

1

(ii) Suggest **one** abiotic factor which affects how well the living organisms break down the sewage over the course of a year.

_____

1

[Turn over

18. An investigation was carried out into the effects of various additives on dough. Yeast was mixed with flour and sugar solution to make dough. The dough was then cut into four pieces and additives were added to three of them. $20 \, cm^3$ of each dough was put into measuring cylinders and the volume of the dough was measured after one hour.

The results are shown below.

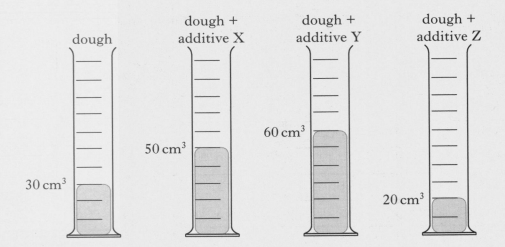

(a) Calculate the percentage increase in the volume of the dough with no additive.

Space for calculation

_____ %

1

(b) What substance produced by yeast caused the dough to rise?

_____

1

(c) Which additive caused the greatest increase in the volume of the dough?

_____

1

(d) Which additive may have prevented the yeast fermenting?

_____

1

(e) What type of organism is yeast?

_____

1

Marks | KU | PS

19. (a) Pollution can affect areas such as fresh water and seas.

Name the **two** other main areas which can be affected by pollution.

1 _____

2 _____

1

(b) Complete the table to show the **three** main sources of pollution and **one** example of a pollutant from each.

Source	Example of pollutant
industry	
	fertilisers
	litter

2

(c) Pollution from the exhausts of vehicles can be a major problem in some cities.

Give **one** way in which this type of pollution can be controlled.

_____

_____

1

[END OF QUESTION PAPER]

[Turn over

SPACE FOR ANSWERS
AND FOR ROUGH WORKING

ADDITIONAL GRID FOR QUESTION 2(*c*)

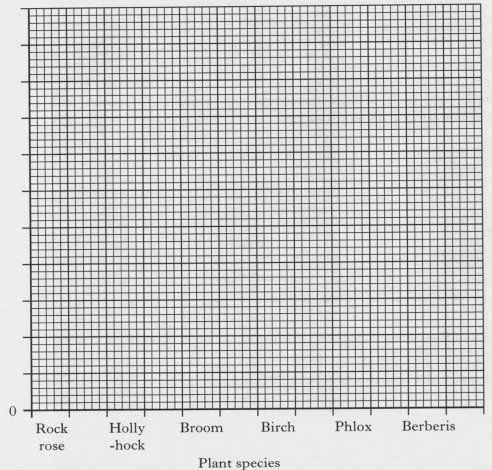

0

Rock   Holly   Broom   Birch   Phlox   Berberis
rose   -hock

Plant species

SPACE FOR ANSWERS
AND FOR ROUGH WORKING

ADDITIONAL GRID FOR QUESTION 9(*a*)

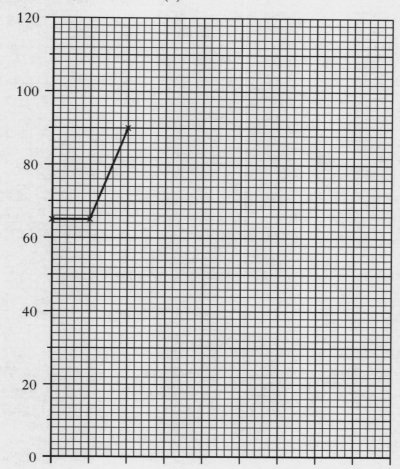

Pulse rate
(beats per
minute)

ADDITIONAL GRID FOR QUESTION 11(*b*)(i)

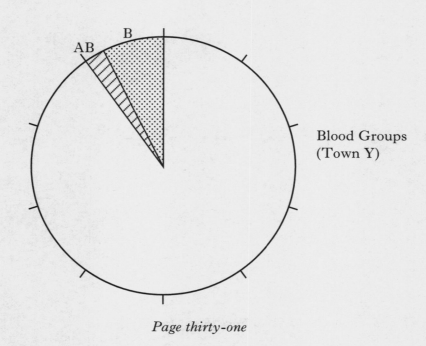

Blood Groups
(Town Y)

SPACE FOR ANSWERS
AND FOR ROUGH WORKING

Page thirty-two

[BLANK PAGE]

FOR OFFICIAL USE

G

KU	PS

Total Marks

0300/401

NATIONAL
QUALIFICATIONS
2006

TUESDAY, 23 MAY
9.00 AM – 10.30 AM

BIOLOGY
STANDARD GRADE
General Level

Fill in these boxes and read what is printed below.

Full name of centre

Town

Forename(s)

Surname

Date of birth
Day Month Year

Scottish candidate number

Number of seat

1 All questions should be attempted.

2 The questions may be answered in any order but all answers are to be written in the spaces provided in this answer book, and must be written clearly and legibly in ink.

3 Rough work, if any should be necessary, as well as the fair copy, is to be written in this book. Additional spaces for answers and for rough work will be found at the end of the book. Rough work should be scored through when the fair copy has been written.

4 Before leaving the examination room you must give this book to the invigilator. If you do not, you may lose all the marks for this paper.

SCOTTISH
QUALIFICATIONS
AUTHORITY

©

1. (a) The grid contains some terms related to the biosphere.

A community	B competition	C ecosystem	D food shortage
E habitat	F light intensity	G population	H predation

Use letters from the grid to complete the following statements.

(i)   An ecosystem is made up of $\boxed{A}$ and $\boxed{E}$.

1

(ii) The interaction between organisms which need the same resources is called $\boxed{B}$.

1

(iii) An example of an abiotic factor is $\boxed{F}$.

1

(b) Describe what is meant by the term *a population*.

~~The amount of~~ all the organisms of one kind

1

1. **(continued)**

(c) The table shows the results of an investigation into the distribution of ling heather and bell heather in an area of moorland.

	Quadrat number				
	1	2	3	4	5
Type of heather present	Ling	Bell	Ling and Bell	Bell	Ling
Soil moisture (units from meter)	4	6	5	7	3
Soil pH	5·6	5·5	5·3	5·6	5·4
Soil temperature (°C)	4	7	8	4	7

(i) Calculate the average soil moisture reading in the investigation area.
Space for calculation

_____5_____ units

1

(ii) The soil pH was measured using a soil pH meter. Describe how the average pH of the soil in a single quadrat is calculated.

_____

_____

1

(iii) Which abiotic factor appears to have the greatest effect on the distribution of the two types of heather? Give a reason for your answer.

Factor _____

Reason _____

_____

1

(iv) The quadrat used was a square wooden frame.
Describe how a quadrat should be used to investigate the plants present in an area.

thrown randomly onto the ground and count the number of plants in that area. Repeat to make results more reliable.

2

2. An investigation into the effect of soil moisture on the germination of seeds was carried out using the apparatus shown below. Seeds were sown evenly over the whole surface of the soil.

The diagram shows the internal detail of the apparatus.

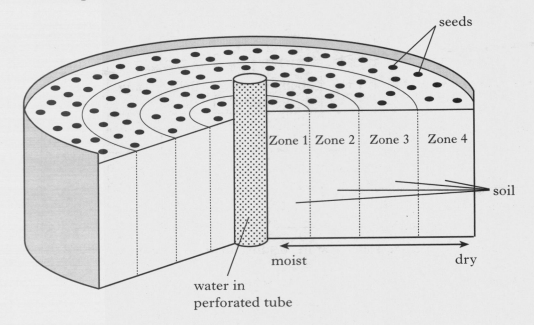

After five days, the percentage of the seeds which had germinated and the average soil moisture in each zone were recorded.

The results are shown in the table.

	Zone 1	Zone 2	Zone 3	Zone 4
Average soil moisture (cm³ per 100 g)	90	70	50	30
Seeds germinated (%)	80	100	72	38

DO NOT WRITE IN THIS MARGIN

Marks | KU | PS

2. **(continued)**

(a) Use the results to complete the bar chart of the germination of the seeds by:

(i) putting the scale on the vertical axis; **1**

(ii) labelling the vertical axis; **1**

(iii) plotting the remaining bars. **1**

(An additional grid, if needed, will be found on page 28.)

(b) (i) From the results in the table, describe the relationship between soil moisture and the percentage of seeds germinated.

the higher the soil moisture is the number of seeds germinated increases. **2**

(ii) Suggest how the investigators could tell whether a seed had germinated.

you will be able to see the root **1**

(iii) Other than soil moisture, name **two** factors which are necessary for the germination of all types of seeds.

1   oxygen

2   warmth **1**

Marks | KU | PS

3. (a) The diagram shows part of a honeysuckle flower.

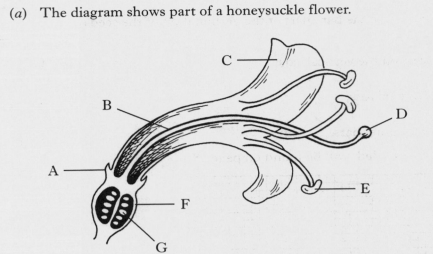

(i) Which letter indicates a structure which produces male gametes?

F

1

(ii) Give the name and function of the structure labelled D.

Name _anthers_

1

Function _collect pollen_

1

(iii) Give the letter and name of the structure which develops into a fruit.

Letter _G_

Name _ovaries / ovule_

1

Marks | KU | PS

3. **(continued)**

(b) (i) The diagram below shows stages in the life cycle of a flowering plant. Use words from the list to complete the diagram.

List: **fertilisation   fruit formation   pollination**

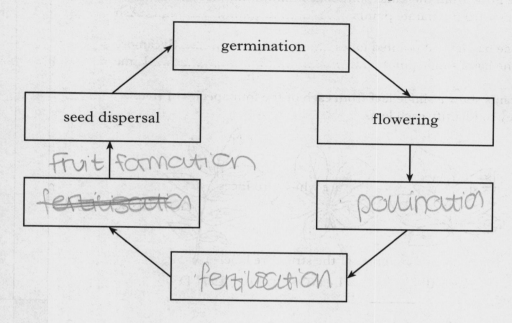

1

(ii) Underline **one** option in each set of brackets to complete the following sentence correctly.

The type of plant reproduction which involves seeds is $\left\{ \begin{array}{c} \text{sexual} \\ \text{asexual} \end{array} \right\}$

and cannot take place without $\left\{ \begin{array}{c} \text{insects} \\ \text{pollination} \end{array} \right\}$.

1

[Turn over

4. The key can be used to identify four species of trees from the shape of their leaves.

1   Leaf divided into a number of separate leaflets.........................Go to 2
      Leaf not divided into separate leaflets.......................................Go to 3

2   All leaflets grow from the same point ....Horse chestnut
      Leaflets grow from separate points ....Ash

3   Leaf outline has several pointed lobes ....Sycamore
      Leaf outline has a single point ....Lime

(*a*) The diagrams show a single leaf from each of the four species of tree. Use the key to identify each leaf.

Leaf A   Leaf B   Leaf C   Leaf D

lime   *sycamore*   *horse chestnut*   *ash*

2

(*b*) Use the same information from the key above to construct a branched key in the outline below.

(An additional outline, if needed, will be found on page 28.)

Tree Leaves

leaf divided into a number of separate leaflets

leaf not divided into separate leaflets

all leaflets grown from the same point

leaflets grown from separate points

Leaf outline has several pointed lobes

leaf outline has a single point

Horse chestnut   *ash*   *sycamore*   *lime*

2

Marks | KU | PS

5. The table gives information about the nutrients found in 100 g of three different breakfast cereals.

	Cereal X	Cereal Y	Cereal Z
Protein (g)	15	10	15
Fat (g)	0	2	5
Carbohydrate (g)	60	65	65
Fibre (g)	10	15	5

(a) (i) Which cereal provides the most energy per 100 g?

Cereal ___~~Z~~ Y___

1

(ii) Calculate the protein : fat : carbohydrate content of Cereal X as a simple whole number ratio.

Space for calculation

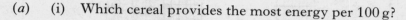

___1___ : ___0___ : ___4___

protein : fat : carbohydrate

1

(iii) Which of the cereals is represented by the following pie chart?

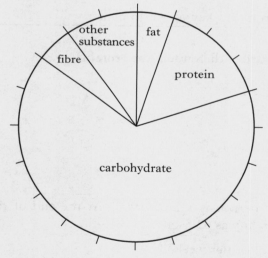

Cereal ___Z___

1

(b) Animals obtain their energy from food.

Give **one** other reason why animals need food.

___to keep them warm___

1

(c) From which part of a mammal's digestive system are digestion products absorbed into the bloodstream?

___liver___

1

6. Loss of fat, protein and water all contribute to the total weight lost by a person on a slimming diet.

The graph shows the changes in the percentages of these in the weight lost during a three week period.

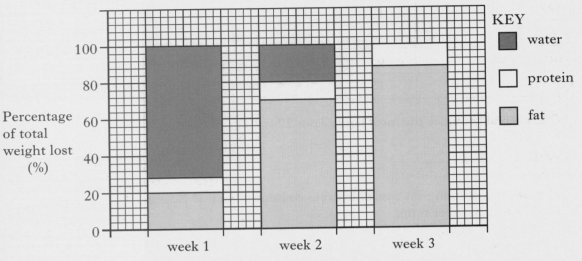

(a) During week 1, which substance accounted for most of the weight lost?

___Water___

1

(b) What happened to the percentage of fat in the weight lost by the person as the diet continued during the three weeks?

___it increased___

1

(c) What percentage of the weight lost each week was protein?

Week 1 __8__ %

Week 2 __10__ %

Week 3 __12__ %

1

(d) Before starting the diet, the person weighed 70 kg. At the end of the three weeks, the person's weight was 62·5 kg.

What was the average weight loss per week?

Space for calculation

2·5

___ kg per week

1

DO NOT WRITE IN THIS MARGIN

Marks	KU	PS

7. The graph shows the activity of enzymes A, B and C at different pH values.

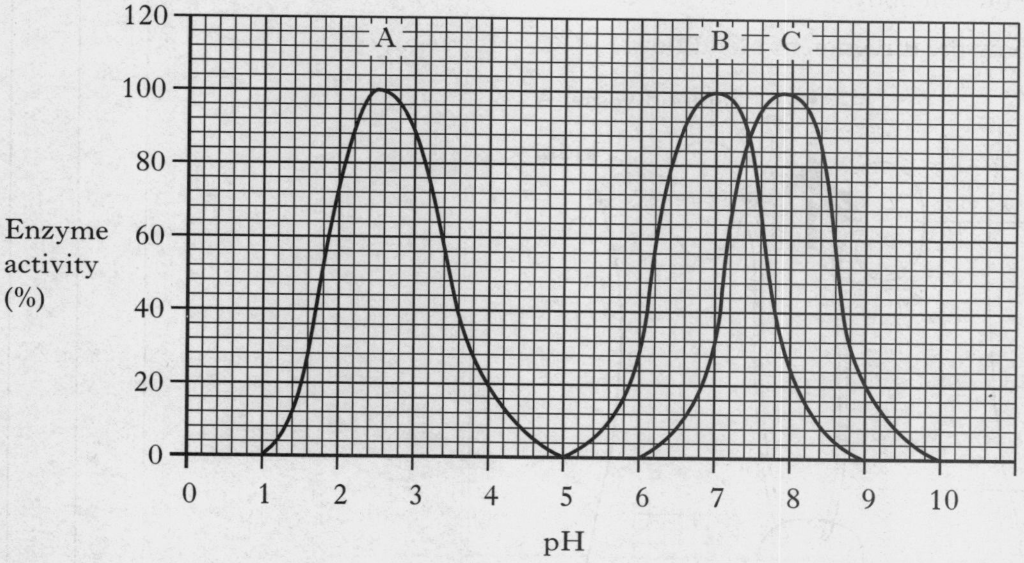

(a) Which enzyme could be pepsin?

Enzyme B **1**

(b) Over what pH range would enzymes B and C **both** be able to work?

Between pH 7 and pH 8 **1**

(c) Describe the changes in the activity of enzyme B as the pH changes from pH 5 to pH 9.

~~it decreases fast~~ it incresses from 5 - 7 then begins to decrease fast **2**

(d) (i) Enzymes are biological catalysts.

Explain the meaning of the word *catalyst*.

____

______________________________ **1**

(ii) What type of chemical substance are enzymes composed of?

______________________________ **1**

[Turn over

Marks | KU | PS

8. (*a*) The diagram below shows part of the system used to regulate water content in the human body.

The arrows show the direction of blood flow.

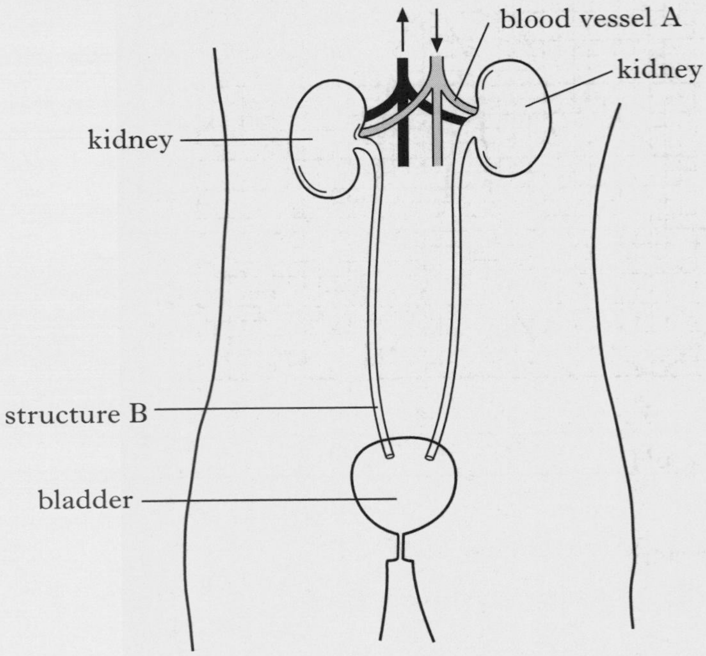

blood vessel A

kidney

kidney

structure B

bladder

(i) Name blood vessel A.

_____

1

(ii) Name structure B.

_____

1

(iii) What is the function of the bladder?

Store urine une _____

1

(iv) Name the toxic waste product removed from the blood by filtration in the kidneys.

_____

1

8. **(continued)**

(b)   The table below shows the daily water gains and losses of a person at three different temperatures.

		Normal temperature	Colder temperature	Warmer temperature
Water gain (cm³)	In drinks	1500	1500	1500
	In food	800	800	800
	From respiration	300	300	300
	TOTAL	2600	2600	2600
Water loss (cm³)	In breath	400	400	600
	In sweat	1000	600	4000
	In urine	1100	1500	500
	In faeces	100	100	100
	TOTAL	2600	2600	5200

(i)   Water balance is usually achieved by the body.

What evidence from the table supports this statement?

all the numbers are the same.

Marks **1**

(ii)   What **two** differences are shown in the table between the body's responses to normal and colder temperatures?

1 _more water loss in urine in cold temprature_

2 _more water loss in sweat in cold temprature_

Marks **1**

(iii)   Complete the table by calculating the missing total volume of water loss in the warmer temperature.

Space for calculation

Marks **1**

(iv)   How would water balance usually be achieved in the warmer temperature?

Marks **1**

[Turn over

Marks | KU | PS

9. (a) The diagram represents a leaf cell from a green plant.

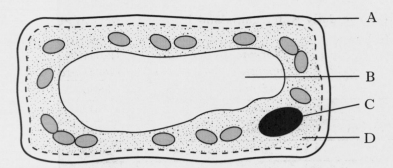

                    A

                    B

                    C

                    D

 (i) Complete the table by naming the parts of the leaf cell.

Label	Part of leaf cell
A	cell wall ~~chloroplast.~~
B	~~vacole~~ cell membrane
C	nucleas
D	~~of~~ cell membrane

2

 (ii) State the function of a cell nucleus.

Controls what enters and
leaves the cell

1

(b) (i) Name **one** substance that can enter a cell by diffusion.

water

1

 (ii) A substance enters a cell by diffusion. What does this indicate about the concentrations of that substance inside and outside the cell?

1

Marks | KU | PS

9. (continued)

(c) A microscope has a choice of three objective lenses. The total magnification depends on the magnifications of the eyepiece lens and the objective lens. Complete the table below to show the magnifications of the microscope.

Eyepiece lens magnification	Objective lens magnification	Total magnification
× 7	× 10	× 70
× 7	× 4	× 140
× 7	× 40	× 280

1

(d) The table below gives information about the size of some cells.

Type of cell	Length of cell (micrometres)
red blood cell	7
human skin cell	20
Elodea leaf cell	80
onion epidermal cell	100

(i) Calculate the length of an onion epidermis cell in millimetres. (1 millimetre = 1000 micrometres)

Space for calculation

_____0·1_____ millimetres

1

(ii) Using information from the table, what general conclusion could be made when comparing animal and plant cells?

_____

1

[Turn over

Page fifteen

Marks | KU | PS

10. Read the passage below.

Likeable Lichens

(adapted from Dobson, F., 2003, "Getting a Liking for Lichens", *Biologist*, 59, 263-267)

Lichens consist of two organisms, a fungus and an alga. Both gain benefit from the association. The fungus forms 90% of the mass of a lichen and provides support and protection. The alga is located in a thin layer just beneath the upper surface. Unlike the fungus, the alga can photosynthesise.

Lichens are found from the hottest desert rocks to the freezing polar regions. About eight percent of the land area of the world is frozen tundra and in such regions lichens are by far the most important photosynthetic organisms. If global warming was to cause a severe reduction in their numbers, the resulting increase of carbon dioxide in the air could be as dangerous to our survival as the loss of the rain forests.

Lichen species differ in their ability to tolerate air pollution. The presence or absence of certain lichens can be used to give a measure of sulphur dioxide levels. In recent years, the level of this pollutant has been falling. Sulphur dioxide emissions in Britain fell by 69% in the ten years from 1990 to 2000. In Kew Gardens in London, the number of species of lichens recorded rose from 6 to 76.

Yellow lichens placed on wounds were known to reduce the chances of infection and saved many lives after battles. It is now known that these lichens contain usnic acid, which has strong anti-bacterial properties. Several antiseptic creams have been produced commercially from this chemical but lichens grow too slowly for large-scale production. Work is proceeding to manufacture similar compounds synthetically.

(*a*) Which types of organism combine to form lichens?

fungus & alga

1

(*b*) Species which can give information about environmental factors are called "indicator species". Select a **complete sentence** from the passage which shows that lichens are useful in this way.

The prescence or absence of certain linchens can be used to give a measure of sulphur dioxide levels.

1

(*c*) Suggest a benefit to the fungus from its association with the photosynthetic alga.

provides

1

DO NOT WRITE IN THIS MARGIN

Marks | KU | PS

10. **(continued)**

(d) Calculate the average yearly increase in the number of lichen species present in Kew Gardens in the ten years from 1990 to 2000.

Space for calculation

6   76

Average increase = _____12.6_____ species per year   **1**

(e) (i) What property of yellow lichens allows them to be used to prevent infections?

_____unsic acid_____   **1**

(ii) What problem prevents the use of lichens for large-scale manufacture of medical products?

_____They grow too slowy_____   **1**

[Turn over

Marks | KU | PS

11. The diagram shows part of the breathing system.

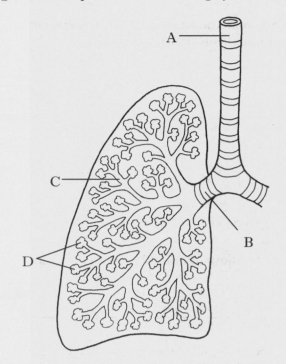

A

C

D

B

(a) Use letters from the diagram to complete the table below.

Structure	Letter
bronchus	B
windpipe	A
air sac	C
bronchiole	D

2

(b) Name the gas which passes from the blood into the lungs to be breathed out.

oxygen

1

Marks | KU | PS

11. (continued)

(c) In an investigation into breathing rates, a pupil had his number of breaths per minute recorded when exercising at different levels.

The procedure was repeated three times and the results are shown in the table below.

	Breathing rate (breaths per minute)			
Exercise	1st Trial	2nd Trial	3rd Trial	Average
standing still	16	15	17	16
walking	19	17	18	18
jogging	27	25	29	27
running quickly	33	31	32	32

(i) Calculate the percentage change in the average breathing rate when running quickly, compared to standing still.

Space for calculation

16
32

_____16_____ % increase   1

(ii) What is the relationship between the level of exercise and breathing rate?

As the exercise increases the breathing rate increases   1

(iii) Why was the investigation repeated three times and an average calculated?

to make the results more reliable.   1

[Turn over

Marks | KU | PS

12. The diagram shows part of the human ear.

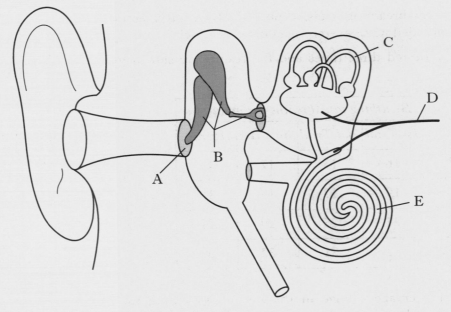

(a) Complete the table to show the name and function of the labelled parts.

Letter	Name	Function
A	ear drum	allows sound into the ear
B	middle ear bones	pass vibrations to inner ear
C	bell	detects movement of the head
E		produces nerve signals
D	auditory nerve	senses

3

Marks | KU | PS

12. **(continued)**

(b) In an investigation, a group of people were asked if they could hear a buzzer. This was repeated at different distances and the percentage of people hearing the buzzer was calculated. The results are shown in the table.

Distance from buzzer (m)	Percentage of people hearing buzzer
5	100
10	98
15	96
20	88
25	74
30	60

On the grid below, complete a **line graph** of the results by:

(i)   labelling the horizontal axis;   **1**

(ii)   adding an appropriate scale to the horizontal axis;   **1**

(iii)   plotting the graph.   **1**

(An additional grid, if needed, will be found on page 29.)

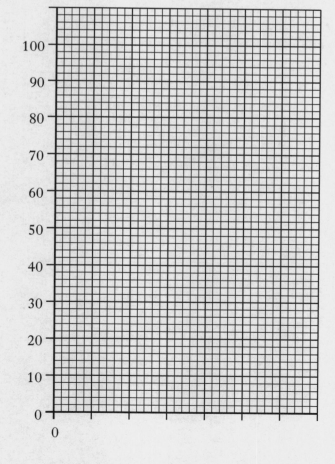

Percentage of people hearing the buzzer

Marks | KU | PS

13. (*a*) The skeleton provides protection for parts of the body.
Give **two** other functions of the skeleton.

1 _____

2 _____   **1**

(*b*) Use lines to link the parts of the skeleton to each of the organs of the body which they protect.

Part of skeleton	*Organs*

rib cage   heart

                            brain

vertebrae   lungs

skull   spinal cord   **2**

Marks KU PS

14. (a) The table below shows the change in the number of cases of three childhood diseases in a population.

Year	Number of cases		
	Measles	Mumps	Rubella
1997	700	180	700
1998	650	155	680
1999	450	150	430
2000	420	110	300
2001	330	90	230
2002	410	150	270

(i) How many children suffered from Rubella in 1999?

_____

1

(ii) Which disease always affected fewer children than the others?

_____

1

(iii) What pattern in the number of cases is shown by all the diseases over the six years of the study?

_____

_____

2

(b) Genetically engineered micro-organisms can be used to make products with medical value. Interferon, used in the treatment of some cancers, can be produced from reprogrammed bacteria, as can human growth hormone which is given to some children to treat pituitary dwarfism. Genetically engineered bacteria are used to produce insulin which is used to treat diabetes. Hepatitis is a liver disease which can be caused by a virus. A vaccine has been developed from genetically engineered yeast cells which helps prevent people becoming infected with the virus.

Complete the table to summarise this information.

Medical condition	Medical product	Type of genetically engineered micro-organism
cancer		
		bacteria
	vaccine	
	insulin	

2

15. (*a*) (i) Complete the diagram to show the sex chromosomes present in the cells of two generations of people.

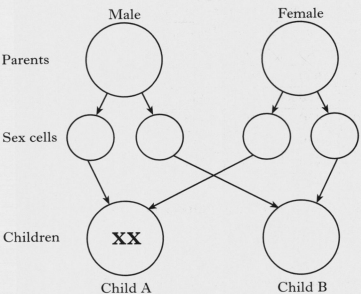

Male Female

Parents

Sex cells

Children   **XX**

Child A Child B

2

(ii) What is the sex of Child A?

_____

1

(*b*) (i) The statements below refer to human sex cells.

Use lines to connect each statement to the correct sex cell.

Statement *Sex cell*

| released in large numbers |

| contains a large food store | | egg |

| produced by the male parent | | sperm |

| moves with the use of a tail |

2

(ii) What is the general name given to sex cells such as eggs and sperm?

_____

1

DO NOT WRITE IN THIS MARGIN

	Marks	KU	PS

15. (continued)

(*c*) How many complete sets of chromosomes are present in a sperm cell?

________________ **1**

(*d*) What name is given to each part of a chromosome which controls a particular characteristic?

________________ **1**

[Turn over

16. The diagram represents one type of sewage treatment works.

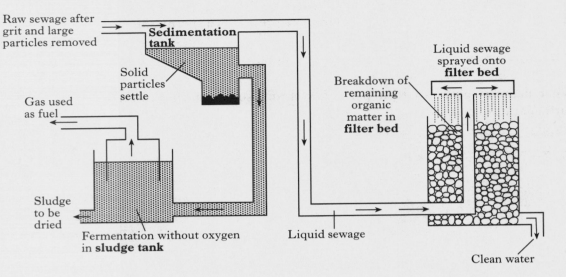

Raw sewage after grit and large particles removed

Sedimentation tank

Solid particles settle

Gas used as fuel

Sludge to be dried

Fermentation without oxygen in **sludge tank**

Breakdown of remaining organic matter in **filter bed**

Liquid sewage sprayed onto **filter bed**

Liquid sewage

Clean water

(*a*) What causes the breakdown of the organic matter in the filter bed?

_____

1

(*b*) The filter bed contains layers of stones and gravel. How does this help to provide the oxygen needed for the breakdown of organic matter?

_____

_____

1

(*c*) (i) Name the gas which is produced in the sludge tank and which can be used as a fuel.

_____

1

(ii) State **one** advantage of using fuels obtained by fermentation rather than fossil fuels.

_____

1

Marks | KU | PS

17. The pH of three different types of milk was measured. After 48 hours in a warm place, the pH was measured again. The results are shown in the table.

Type of milk	pH at start	pH after 48 hours
unpasteurised	6·9	4·2
pasteurised	7·0	5·9
ultra heat treated	6·9	6·0

The production of acid causes the milk to become sour.

(a) Which type of milk was the most sour after 48 hours?

_____

1

(b) Pasteurisation and ultra heat treatment kill bacteria in milk.

What effect do these processes have on the souring of milk?

_____

1

(c) Predict the pH of the pasteurised milk if it had been kept in a colder place for 48 hours.

Tick the correct box

☐   7·5

☐   7·0

☐   6·4

☐   5·5

1

(d) Underline one word in the brackets to complete the following sentence correctly.

Souring of milk is an example of a $\left\{\begin{array}{l}\text{digestion} \\ \text{synthesis} \\ \text{fermentation}\end{array}\right\}$ reaction.

1

[*END OF QUESTION PAPER*]

[Turn over

     Page twenty-seven

SPACE FOR ANSWERS
AND FOR ROUGH WORKING

ADDITIONAL GRID FOR QUESTION 2(*a*)

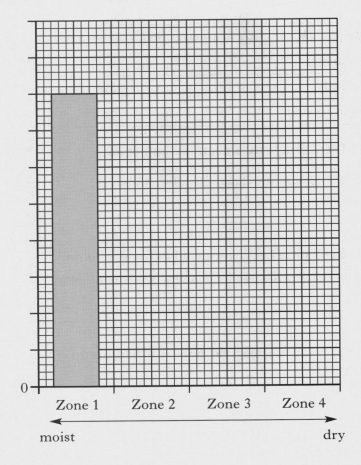

ADDITIONAL KEY OUTLINE FOR QUESTION 4(*b*)

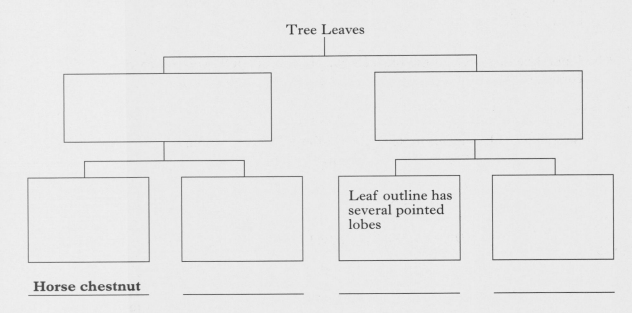

SPACE FOR ANSWERS
AND FOR ROUGH WORKING

ADDITIONAL GRID FOR QUESTION 12(b)

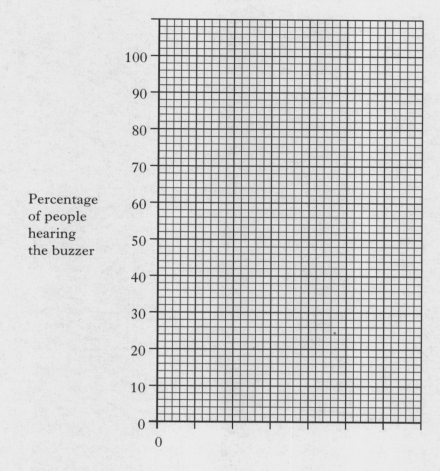

SPACE FOR ANSWERS
AND FOR ROUGH WORKING

[BLANK PAGE]

[BLANK PAGE]

FOR OFFICIAL USE

KU	PS
32	44

Total Marks

0300/401

NATIONAL
QUALIFICATIONS
2007

MONDAY, 21 MAY
9.00 AM – 10.30 AM

BIOLOGY
STANDARD GRADE
General Level

Fill in these boxes and read what is printed below.

Full name of centre

Town

Forename(s)

Surname

Date of birth
Day Month Year   Scottish candidate number   Number of seat

1 All questions should be attempted.

2 The questions may be answered in any order but all answers are to be written in the spaces provided in this answer book, and must be written clearly and legibly in ink.

3 Rough work, if any should be necessary, as well as the fair copy, is to be written in this book. Additional spaces for answers and for rough work will be found at the end of the book. Rough work should be scored through when the fair copy has been written.

4 Before leaving the examination room you must give this book to the invigilator. If you do not, you may lose all the marks for this paper.

SCOTTISH
QUALIFICATIONS
AUTHORITY

1. The diagram shows a food web from a moorland ecosystem.

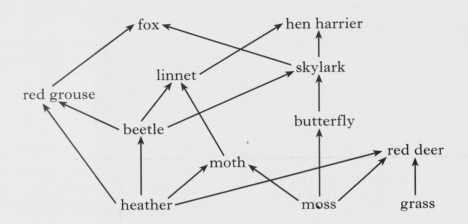

(a) The following statements refer to the food web.

Complete the table by entering "**T**" when the statement is true, and "**F**" when the statement is false.

Statement	T or F
Linnets are eaten by beetles and moths.	F
Foxes and hen harriers are not eaten by anything.	T
Butterflies are eaten by skylarks which are eaten by foxes.	T

1

(b) Give an example of a producer and a consumer from the food web.

Producer *grass*

Consumer *red deer*

1

(c) Which plant provides energy for the greatest number of different species in this food web?

heather

1

(d) Give **two** ways in which energy can be lost from this food web.

1 *facess*

2 *death*

2

Marks | KU | PS

2. (*a*) The phrases below refer to man's influence on natural resources.

1   Overgrazing by too many animals in one area
2   Air pollution by sulphur dioxide released by burning fossil fuels
3   Overfishing by modern fishing boats

Choose **one** of the phrases and describe a problem which may result from it.

Phrase number ___1___

Problem ___food will dissappear___ ___and animals will not consume___ ___enough food.___

1

(*b*) The diagram shows the position of a food-processing factory beside a river.

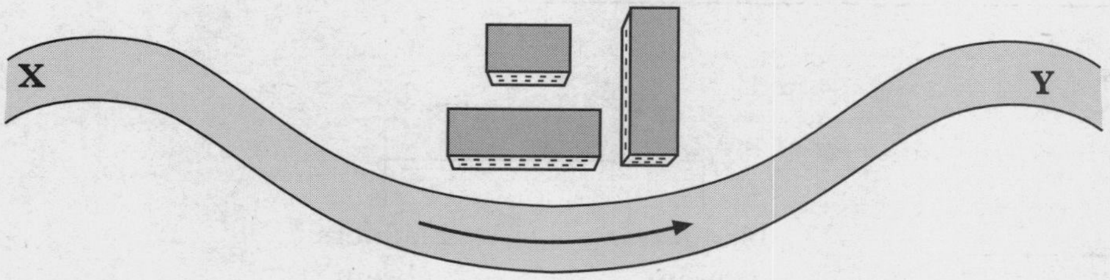

food-processing factory

X

Y

direction of river flow

The factory accidentally released organic waste into the river.

Water samples were taken from points **X** and **Y** and analysed for the numbers of micro-organisms and oxygen concentration.

(i) Complete the following sentence by <u>underlining</u> the correct word in each bracket.

Water samples from point **X** had $\left\{ \begin{array}{c} \text{more} \\ \underline{\text{fewer}} \end{array} \right\}$ micro-organisms and a $\left\{ \begin{array}{c} \underline{\text{higher}} \\ \text{lower} \end{array} \right\}$ oxygen concentration than samples from point **Y**.

1

(ii) What does the organic waste provide for the micro-organisms in the river?

___food___

1

[Turn over

Official SQA Past Papers: General Biology 2007

DO NOT
WRITE IN
THIS
MARGIN

Marks | KU | PS

3. Some features of common seaweeds are shown in the table below.

Seaweed	Colour	Shape	Bladders
Bladder wrack	brown	branched	in pairs
Channel wrack	brown	grooved	absent
Cladophora	green	long and thin	absent
Egg wrack	brown	branched	along its length
Sea lettuce	green	flat	absent
Serrated wrack	brown	saw-toothed edges	absent
Spiral wrack	brown	twisted	in pairs

(a) (i) Use the information in the table to complete the key below by writing the correct feature on each dotted line and the correct seaweed names in the empty boxes.

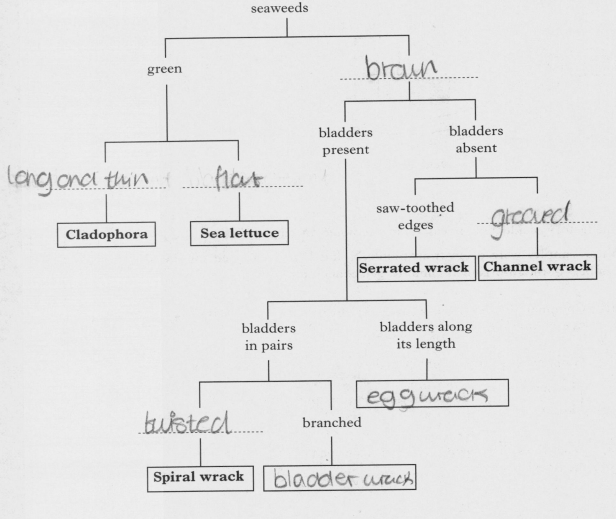

3

Marks | KU | PS

3. **(a)** **(continued)**

(ii) Describe **two** differences between Sea lettuce and Spiral wrack.

1 colour - Sea lettuce is green, spiral wrack is

2 shape - Sea lettuce is brown flat, spiral wreck is twisted.

1

(iii) Describe the features which Bladder wrack and Spiral wrack have in common.

bladders are present and in pairs.

1

(b) Abiotic factors can affect the community of seaweeds that grow on a rocky shore.

Identify **two** abiotic factors from the list below.

Tick (✓) the correct boxes

temperature ☑

competition ☑

light intensity ☑

grazing by limpets ☐

disease ☐

1

[Turn over

Marks | KU | PS

4. There are four major groups of plants. Features used to identify members of each group include the presence of a transport system, the shape of their leaves and their method of reproduction.

Flowering plants and the conifers reproduce using seeds. They both have transport systems but they differ in the shape of their leaves. Conifers have needle-like leaves whereas the leaves of flowering plants are either narrow or broad. Mosses don't have any true leaves or transport systems. Ferns have transport systems and feathery leaves but they reproduce using spores, as do the mosses.

(a) Use the information above to complete the table about the plant groups.

Plant group	Transport system	Leaves	Structures used in reproduction
mosses	absent	no true leaves	spores
Ferns	present	feathery	spores
Conifers	present	needle-like	seeds
flowering plants	present	narrow or broad	seeds

3

(b) One type of transport system in plants carries water from the roots to the leaves.

(i) Name the type of tissue involved in this transport system.

stem

1

(ii) Describe a function of a different transport system in plants.

1

(c) Some plants are useful to humans.

State a use by humans of a named plant.

Plant   poppy

Use   to make morphine

1

5. The diagrams show two natural methods of asexual reproduction in flowering plants.

Method A

Method B

Strawberry plant

Potato plant

X

(a) Name the two methods of asexual reproduction.

Method A _manval_

Method B _wind_

(b) What does structure **X** contribute to the growth of a new potato plant?

it stores the food for the plant

(c) Name an artificial method of propagating flowering plants.

_____

[Turn over

Marks	KU	PS
2	0	
1	1	
1	0	

6. The chart shows the times when different vegetable crops can be sown and harvested.

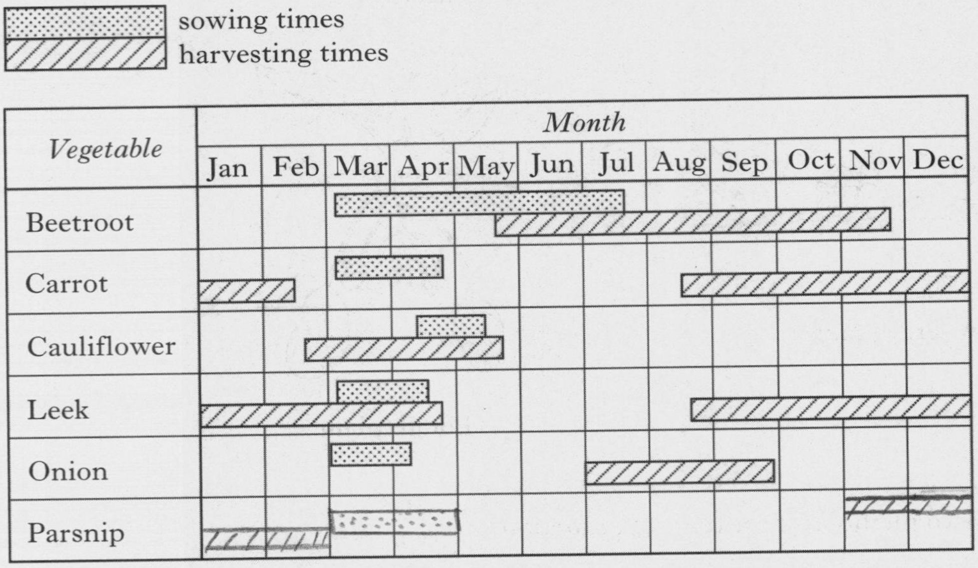

	sowing times
	harvesting times

Vegetable	Month											
	Jan	Feb	Mar	Apr	May	Jun	Jul	Aug	Sep	Oct	Nov	Dec
Beetroot												
Carrot												
Cauliflower												
Leek												
Onion												
Parsnip												

(a) Parsnip seeds can be sown throughout March and April. The parsnip crop can be harvested from the beginning of November to the end of February.

Add this information to the chart.

(An additional chart will be found, if needed, on page 28.)

2

(b) During which month is it possible to sow seeds for all the vegetables?

April

1

(c) Which crop can be harvested over the longest period of time?

Leek

1

(d) Name **all** the crops which could be harvested in the same month as seeds of the same species are being sown.

beetroot, cauliflower, leek

1

DO NOT WRITE IN THIS MARGIN

Marks	KU	PS
2		2
1		1
1		1
1		1

7. (a) An investigation was set up to examine the behaviour of slugs.

Food

During the investigation the slugs moved towards the food.

(i) Two possible hypotheses for the movement of the slugs are:

1 The slugs saw the food and moved towards it.

2 The slugs smelled the food and moved towards it.

How could the investigation be improved to show which hypothesis was correct?

place the food behind the slugs instead of unfront of them.

(ii) Why was it good experimental practice to use several slugs rather than just one?

to make your results more reliable.

(b) Give **one** example of an abiotic factor which can affect the behaviour of a named animal and describe the response of the animal to that factor.

Animal _____ Abiotic factor_____

Response _____

_____

[Turn over

8. (*a*) The diagram shows the skulls of two mammals.

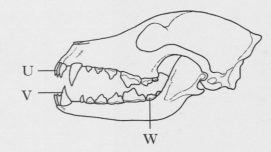 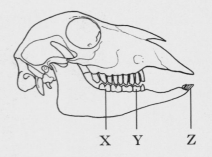

Use letters from the diagram to identify the following teeth.

(i) Incisors _____V_____ and _____Z_____   **1**

(ii) A tooth used for piercing and holding prey _____V_____ **1**

(iii) A tooth used for crushing and grinding plant material

_____X_____   **1**

(*b*) The diagram below shows the human digestive system.

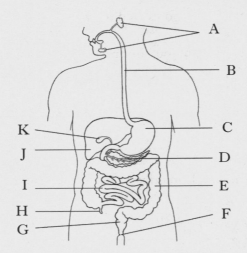

(i) Complete the table to identify the following parts of the digestive system.

Part of digestive system	Letter
oesophagus	B
pancreas	D
Gall bladder	K
Stomach	C

2

DO NOT WRITE IN THIS MARGIN

Marks | KU | PS

8. (*b*) (continued)

(ii) What is the main function of part E of the diagram?

re Absorb water — 1 | 1

(*c*) The diagram shows a cross section of the small intestine.

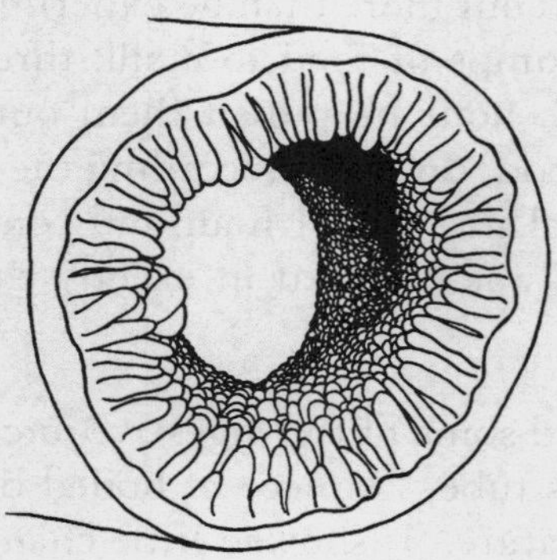

Describe **one** feature of the small intestine shown on the diagram and explain how it helps in the absorption of food.

Feature folded

Explanation larger surface area for reabsorbtion of water — 1 | 1

[Turn over

Marks | KU | PS

9. Read the following passage and answer the questions based on it.

Alexis St. Martin – Human Guinea Pig

In 1822, a 20 year old Canadian fur trapper called Alexis St. Martin was accidentally injured by a shotgun. His abdomen and stomach were blasted open. He survived thanks to prompt treatment by a local doctor. His stomach did not fully heal and Alexis was left with an opening to his stomach which the doctor covered with a leather flap.

The doctor was a keen scientist and carried out more than 60 experiments on his patient. In one experiment he tied lumps of food to a silk thread and pushed them into Alexis' stomach. Each hour he pulled them out to see what the stomach juices had done to the food, carefully recording the results. A piece of boiled beef was half the original size after 1 hour and completely gone after 2 hours. A piece of raw beef was digested in exactly the same manner.

In another experiment, the doctor removed some of the digestive juices from Alexis' stomach and put them into a glass tube. A piece of boiled beef was put into the tube and kept at body temperature. It showed little change after 1 hour, was only half gone in 2 hours and disappeared after 4 hours.

Despite his injuries Alexis led a long and healthy life. He married and had six children. He survived to the age of 86, outliving the doctor by many years.

(a) What was the purpose of the silk thread?

So that you can pull the lumps of food back out again

1 | | 1

(b) Why did the doctor keep the experiment in the glass tube at body temperature?

Its the optimum temprature for enzymes to work

1 | | 1

(c) How long did Alexis live after the shotgun accident?
Space for calculation

86
- 20
66

_____66_____ years

1 | | 1

Marks | KU | PS

9. (continued)

(d) Use information from the passage to complete the table of results.

		Raw beef in stomach	Boiled beef in stomach	Boiled beef in glass tube
	0	unaffected	unaffected	unaffected
Time (hours)	1	affected	half the size	little change
	2	digested	completely gone	half gone
	4	digestion complete	digestion complete	digestion complete

2

1

[Turn over

DO NOT WRITE IN THIS MARGIN

Marks | KU | PS

10. (a) (i) What effect does cell division have on the number of cells in the human body?

increases

1

(ii) What part of a cell controls cell division?

nucleas

1

(b) The following phrases describe stages in cell division.

Stage P—Chromosomes line up at the equator of the cell.

Stage Q—Nuclear membranes form and cytoplasm divides.

Stage R—Chromatids separate and move to opposite ends of the cell.

Stage S—Each chromosome doubles itself and appears as coiled threads.

Use the letters to arrange the stages into the correct order.

First stage   S

Second stage   P

Third stage   Q

Fourth stage   R

1

(c) A cell divides every 20 minutes. How many cells would be produced from one original cell at the end of two hours?

Space for calculation

91 cells

1

Marks | KU | PS

11. The graph shows the maximum recommended pulse rate for humans of different ages.

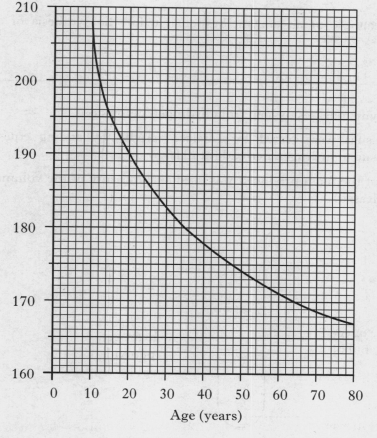

Maximum recommended pulse rate (beats per minute)

Age (years)

(a) What is the maximum recommended pulse rate for a person aged 15 years?

_____ 195 beats per minute

1

(b) At what age does the maximum recommended pulse rate fall below 200 beats per minute?

above _____ 12 years

1

(c) Calculate the percentage decrease in the maximum recommended pulse rate between the ages of 20 and 60 years.

Space for calculation

$$\frac{190}{171}$$

$$\frac{19}{190}$$

_____ 10 %

1

Marks | KU | PS

12. (a) All living cells require enzymes. What would happen to chemical reactions in a cell if enzymes were not present?

the reactions would be slow for anything to work.

1

(b) Give **one** example of an enzyme responsible for the synthesis of a substance.

amylase

1

(c) Catalase enzyme releases oxygen from hydrogen peroxide.

Different tissues were tested for catalase activity by adding equal masses of tissue to hydrogen peroxide at pH 7.

The height of the foam produced was used as a measure of the volume of oxygen released.

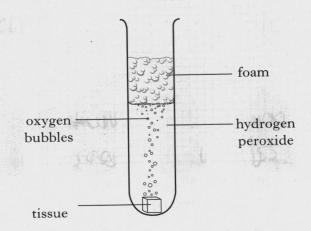

foam

oxygen bubbles

hydrogen peroxide

tissue

The results are shown in the table.

Type of tissue	Height of foam (mm)
apple	24
potato	28
beef	53
carrot	22
fish	48
chicken	50

(i) Give **one** variable, other than pH, which must be kept constant in this investigation.

the volume of hydrogen peroxide

1

Marks | KU | PS

12. (c) **(continued)**

(ii) Use the information in the table to complete the bar chart by:

1 adding a scale to the y-axis; **1**

2 labelling the y-axis; **1**

3 drawing the bars. **1**

(An additional grid will be found, if needed, on page 28.)

(iii) Beef, fish and chicken tissues produced greater volumes of oxygen than the others.

Suggest a hypothesis which could explain this fact.

they are meat

1

(iv) The investigation was carried out at pH7.

Use the words **increase**, **decrease** or **stay the same** to complete the following sentence correctly.

At pH 4 oxygen production would _decrease_ and

at pH 11 oxygen production would _increase_ .

1

[Turn over

Marks | KU | PS

13. (a) The diagram shows part of a human skeleton.

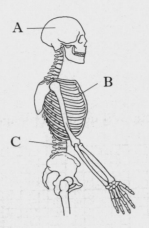

Complete the table below to name each part of the skeleton labelled on the diagram and name **one** organ protected by that part.

Letter	Part of skeleton	Organ protected
A	skull	brain
B	rib cage	lungs
C	spinal cord	spine

2

(b) Complete the table below by inserting ticks (✓) to say whether each line refers to a hinge joint, a ball and socket joint or both types of joint.

	Hinge	Ball and socket
shoulder joint		✓
knee joint	✓	
hip joint		✓
elbow joint	✓	
can move in only one plane	✓	
can move in many planes		✓
held together by ligaments		✓
cartilage protects the ends of the bones	✓	✓

3

DO NOT WRITE IN THIS MARGIN

Marks | KU | PS

13. (continued)

(c) The diagram shows some of the muscles in a human leg.

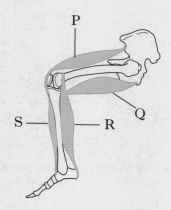

(i) Which muscle contracts to straighten the leg?

___P___

1

(ii) What is the name of the structures which attach the muscles to bones?

___tendon s___

1

[Turn over

Official SQA Past Papers: General Biology 2007

DO NOT
WRITE IN
THIS
MARGIN

Marks | KU | PS

14. (*a*) The diagram shows a human eye.

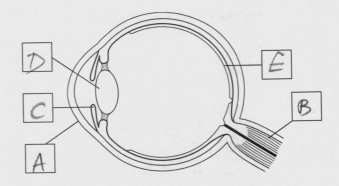

Use the information in the table below to add the correct letters to the diagram.

Letter	Description
A	cornea
B	optic nerve
C	controls the amount of light entering the eye
D	changes shape to adjust focus
E	converts light to electrical impulses

2

(*b*) The diagram shows an investigation into the judgement of distance.

Volunteers each threw 10 hoops at a peg 3 metres away. The number of successful throws was recorded. Each volunteer attempted the test three times, once using the right eye only, once using the left eye only and once using both eyes.

The results are shown in the following chart.

14. **(b)** **(continued)**

right eye only ▓ left eye only ■ both eyes ▨

Number of successes per ten throws

(i) Calculate the average number of successful throws by the volunteers for each trial.

Space for calculations

2+ 3+ 2+ 4+ 4
= 15 ÷ 5 = 3

Average number of successful throws using right eye only ___3___.

Average number of successful throws using left eye only ___2___.

Average number of successful throws using both eyes ___6___.

(ii) Suggest **two** valid conclusions about the distance judgement of the volunteers which can be drawn from the results.

1 More people have successful throws using both eyes

2 people have less successful throws using their left eye only'

(iii) The brain, spinal cord and nerves are all involved in such activities. What is the collective name for these parts of the body?

the central nervous system

15. (*a*) The diagrams below show the inheritance of the sex chromosomes **X** and **Y**.

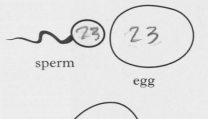

sperm   egg   sperm   egg

XY   XX

fertilised egg   fertilised egg

Sex __male__   Sex __female__

Complete the diagrams by:

(i) inserting the missing sex chromosomes into the eggs and sperm;   **1**

(ii) writing the sex of each fertilised egg in the spaces provided.   **1**

(*b*) Complete the following sentences by <u>underlining</u> the correct word in each bracket.

The name given to a group of interbreeding organisms which produce

fertile young is a $\left\{ \begin{array}{l} \text{tissue} \\ \text{clone} \\ \underline{\text{species}} \end{array} \right\}$.

Characteristics of offspring are controlled by $\left\{ \begin{array}{l} \text{enzymes} \\ \underline{\text{genes}} \\ \text{phenotype} \end{array} \right\}$.   **2**

(*c*) (i) Down's Syndrome is an example of a condition caused by a change to the chromosomes.

What is the correct term for a change to the chromosomes?

__mutation__   **1**

(ii) Down's Syndrome can be detected before birth by the removal of some of the fluid surrounding the baby as it develops. The fluid is removed by a doctor using a syringe inserted into the uterus.

What name is given to this procedure?

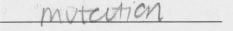
__amniostefis__   **1**

15. (continued)

(*d*) The following table shows the risk to women of different ages of having a baby with Down's Syndrome.

Woman's age (years)	Risk of Down's Syndrome (per 10 000 births)
18	4
22	6
28	8
32	12
38	34
42	100

(i) How many times greater is the risk to a 42 year old woman of having a Down's Syndrome baby, compared to an 18 year old woman?

Space for calculation.

4 : 100

__25__ times greater

1

(ii) Complete the line graph below by:

1 completing the scale on the *y*-axis;

1

2 adding a label to the *y*-axis;

1

3 plotting the graph.

1

(An additional grid will be found, if needed, on page 29.)

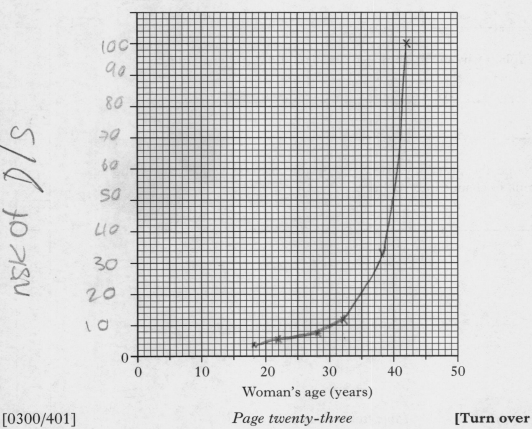

Marks | KU | PS

16. In an investigation into the conditions required for making yoghurt, the following steps were carried out.

1 Milk was pasteurised by heating to over 75 °C.

2 Yoghurt-making bacteria were added to the milk and the mixture was stirred.

3 Four samples were taken and kept at different temperatures.

4 The pH of each sample was measured every hour.

The results are shown in the following table.

Temperature (°C)	pH of sample					
	Start	1 hour	2 hours	3 hours	4 hours	5 hours
5	7·0	7·0	7·0	7·0	7·0	7·0
20	7·0	6·8	6·5	6·0	5·4	4·8
35	7·0	6·5	5·9	5·2	4·4	3·5
50	7·0	7·0	7·0	7·0	7·0	7·0

(a) (i) What precaution was taken to ensure that no harmful bacteria were present in the milk at the start?

it was pasteurised by heating to over 75°c

1

(ii) From the results, what is the optimum temperature for yoghurt production?

5 °C

1

(iii) Explain why the mixture kept at 50 °C did not change in pH.

its reached its optimum

1

(iv) Name the process carried out by the bacteria which causes the milk to change into yoghurt.

1

Marks | KU | PS

16. **(continued)**

(b) The table shows how the fat content of the yoghurt varies according to the type of milk used to make it.

Type of milk used	Fat content of yoghurt (%)
whole	over 3·0
semi-skimmed	0·5–3·0
skimmed	under 0·5

The following table shows the fat and lactose content of three yoghurts.

Yoghurt	Composition	
	fat (%)	lactose (%)
A	2·8	3·9
B	4·0	4·5
C	0·4	3·0

(i) Using information from both tables, identify which yoghurt was made from:

1 semi-skimmed milk   yoghurt ___C___

2 whole milk   yoghurt ___B___   1   0

(ii) What is the range of lactose concentrations in the yoghurts?

From __3·0__ to __4·5__ %   1   1

[Turn over

Marks | KU | PS

17. (a) The following bar chart shows the incidence of diabetes in people of different ages.

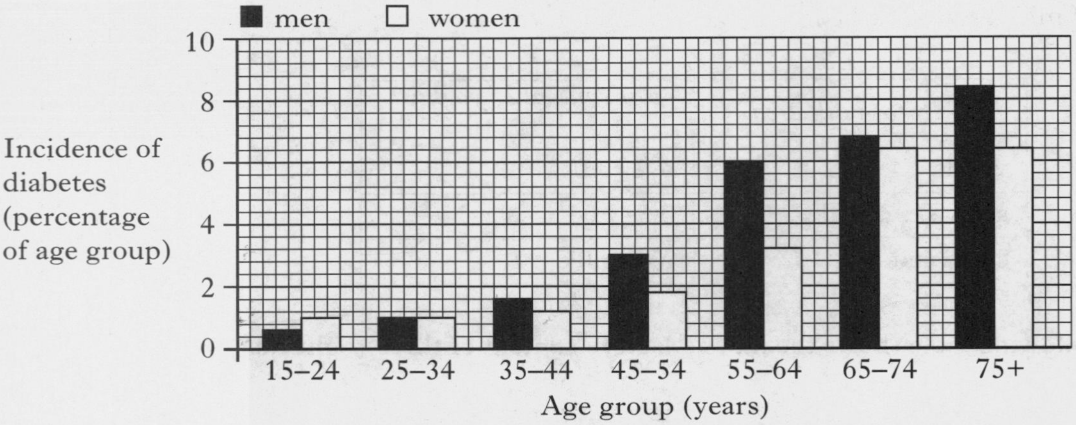

Incidence of diabetes (percentage of age group)

Age group (years)

men   women

(i) Which age group has the highest incidence of diabetes?

_75+_ years

1

(ii) What is the incidence of diabetes in the following groups?

A men aged between 35 and 44   _1·4_ % 1·6

B women aged between 55 and 64 _3·4_ %

1

(iii) What age group shows no difference in the incidence of diabetes in men and women?

_25-34_ years

1

(b) (i) Diabetes can be treated with a substance produced by genetic engineering. Name this substance.

Insulin

1

(ii) What type of chemical, used in biological washing powders, can be produced by genetic engineering?

_____

1

(iii) During genetic engineering, what is transferred into bacteria from another organism?

_____

1

Marks | KU | PS

18. The eye colours of 160 school pupils are shown in the table below.

Eye colour	Number of school pupils
brown	80
green	24
blue	48
grey	8

(a) Complete the pie chart to show this information.

(An additional chart will be found, if needed, on page 29.)

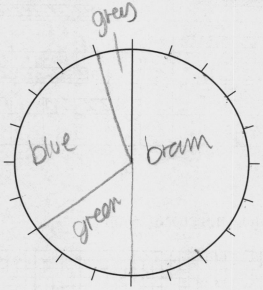

2

2

(b) What type of variation is shown by eye colour?

discontinous

1

1

(c) What percentage of the school pupils had green eyes?

Space for calculation

$\dfrac{24}{160} \times 100$

_____15____ %

1

1

[END OF QUESTION PAPER]

SPACE FOR ANSWERS
AND FOR ROUGH WORKING

ADDITIONAL CHART FOR QUESTION 6(a)

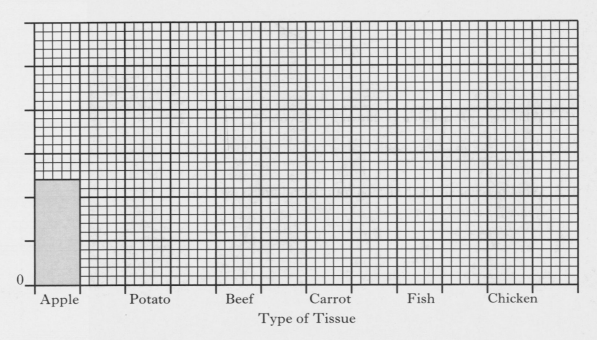

sowing times
harvesting times

Vegetable	Month											
	Jan	Feb	Mar	Apr	May	Jun	Jul	Aug	Sep	Oct	Nov	Dec
Beetroot			▒	▒	▒	▒ ▨	▨	▨	▨	▨	▨	
Carrot	▨	▨	▒	▒				▨	▨	▨	▨	▨
Cauliflower			▨	▨ ▒	▨ ▒							
Leek	▨	▨	▨ ▒	▨ ▒					▨	▨	▨	▨
Onion			▒	▒			▨	▨	▨			
Parsnip												

ADDITIONAL GRAPH PAPER FOR QUESTION 12(c)(ii)

Type of Tissue

Apple   Potato   Beef   Carrot   Fish   Chicken

SPACE FOR ANSWERS
AND FOR ROUGH WORKING

ADDITIONAL GRAPH PAPER FOR QUESTION 15(*d*)(ii)

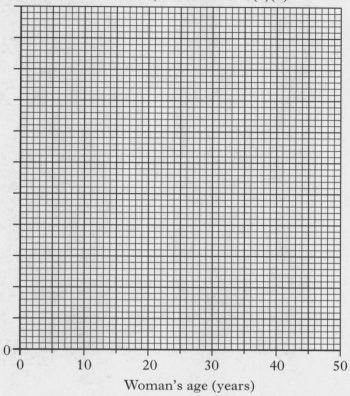

Woman's age (years)

ADDITIONAL CHART PAPER FOR QUESTION 18(*a*)

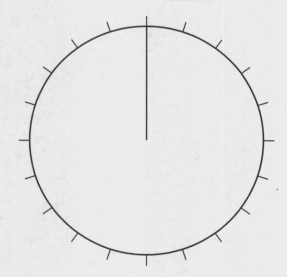

SPACE FOR ANSWERS
AND FOR ROUGH WORKING

[BLANK PAGE]

G

FOR OFFICIAL USE

KU	PS

Total Marks

0300/401

NATIONAL
QUALIFICATIONS
2008

TUESDAY, 27 MAY
9.00 AM – 10.30 AM

BIOLOGY
STANDARD GRADE
General Level

Fill in these boxes and read what is printed below.

Full name of centre

Town

Forename(s)

Surname

Date of birth

Day	Month	Year	Scottish candidate number	Number of seat

1 All questions should be attempted.

2 The questions may be answered in any order but all answers are to be written in the spaces provided in this answer book, and must be written clearly and legibly in ink.

3 Rough work, if any should be necessary, as well as the fair copy, is to be written in this book. Additional spaces for answers and for rough work will be found at the end of the book. Rough work should be scored through when the fair copy has been written.

4 Before leaving the examination room you must give this book to the invigilator. If you do not, you may lose all the marks for this paper.

Marks | KU | PS

1. (a) The key gives information about some water plants growing in a pond.

1 Plant is fully submerged in water ....Go to 2
Plant has leaves on or above surface....................................Go to 3

2 Grows in deep water ....*Elodea*
Grows in shallow water..*Starwort*

3 Plant has roots in soil...Go to 4
Plant is free floating on water surface ....*Water hyacinth*

4 Long and thin leaves ....*Water hawthorn*
Round leaves..Go to 5

5 Resistant to frost..*Water lily*
Cannot survive frost ....*Lotus*

(i) Use the key to identify the plant from the photograph and its description.

Photograph

Description

The plant has its roots in the soil at the bottom of the pond and does not tolerate frost very well.

Name of plant ___~~Lotus~~ Water hawthorn.___   **1**

(ii) Which plant grows submerged in deep water?

___Elodea___   **1**

(iii) Give **three** features that the Water lily and the Lotus have in common.

1 ___round leaves_____

2 _____

3 _____   **2**

1. (continued)

(b) Use words from the list to complete the following sentences.

List   population   community   habitat

A pond provides a ___habitat___ for a

___community___ of many different types of organisms.

Plants of the same species form a ___population___.   **1**

(c) The food web shows the feeding relationships of some of the organisms in a pond.

(i) What do the arrows in the food web represent?

___the direction of energy___   **1**

(ii) A predator is an animal which hunts and kills other animals for food.

Give the names of **two** predators from the food web.

1 ___water beetle___

2 ___stickleback___   **1**

[Turn over

2. Yeast cells were grown and their numbers recorded over a 35 hour period. The results are shown on the graph.

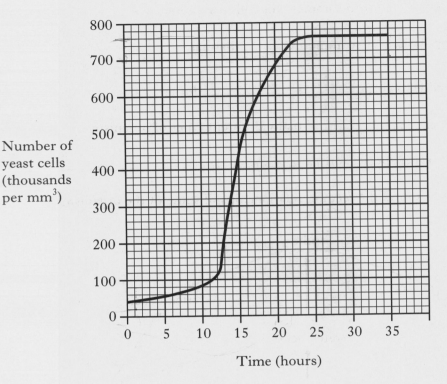

(a) How many times greater was the maximum number of yeast cells compared to the number at the start?

Space for calculation.

760
40

~~~~~~~~~ 19 _____ times greater   **1**

(b) In terms of birth rate and death rate, explain why the population of yeast increased during the first 20 hours.

the birth rate was greater than the death rate   **1**

(c) Name **two** factors which could limit the growth of the population of yeast cells after 20 hours.

1 lack of food

2 lack of oxygen   **2**

Marks | KU | PS

3. The activity of soil organisms was investigated. Some leaves were placed in bags of different mesh sizes and buried in soil for three months.

Each bag was dug up at one month intervals and the percentage decomposition of the leaves recorded. The results are shown on the graph.

Percentage decomposition of the leaves (y-axis, 0–70)
Time (months) (x-axis, 0–3)
large mesh, medium mesh, small mesh

(a) After three months, what percentage of the leaves had decomposed in each bag?

Large mesh bag _____60_____ %

Medium mesh bag _____14_____ %

Small mesh bag _____8_____ %   1

(b) Give **one** feature of the bags and **one** feature of the leaves which would have to be kept constant when setting up the investigation.

Bags _____type of mesh_____   1

Leaves _____type of leaf_____   1

(c) Why was it necessary to wait for one month before collecting any results?

_____allow time of decompisition_____

_____   1

(d) Explain why it is important that leaves and other dead material decompose.

_____returns minerals to the soil_____

_____   1

Marks | KU | PS

4. (*a*) The diagram shows the internal structure of a broad bean seed.

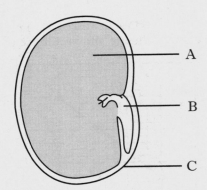

        —— A

        —— B

        —— C

Which letter indicates the food store of the seed?

_____ A _____

1

(*b*) From the list below, <u>underline</u> **two** factors needed for all seeds to germinate.

List   water   carbon dioxide   light   <u>oxygen</u>

1

5. (a) Complete the word equation for photosynthesis.

raw materials	light energy	products
carbon dioxide + glucose	→	water + oxygen

(b) One of the products of photosynthesis may be converted into a storage carbohydrate in the plant. Name this storage carbohydrate.

    Starch

(c) Plants exchange gases with the air during photosynthesis.

Name the openings which allow gases to pass into and out of the leaf.

    Stomata

(d) What substance in green leaves absorbs the light energy for photosynthesis?

    Chlorophyll

[Turn over

6. The graph shows the average wheat yields in the USA and in Europe from 1750 to 2000.

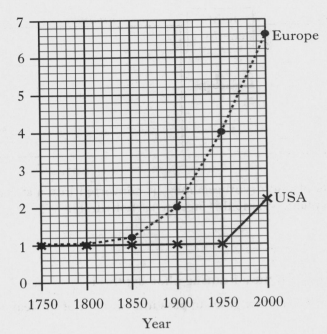

Average
wheat yield
(tonnes/hectare)

Year

(*a*) Describe the pattern of average wheat yield for the USA from 1750 to 2000.

at 1 tonne/hectare
Keeps constant up until 1950 where it
increases to 2.2 tonnes/hectare

2

(*b*) During which 50 year period was there the greatest increase in average wheat yield in Europe?

from ___1950___ to ___2000___

1

(*c*) Calculate the simple whole number ratio of average wheat yield in Europe to that in the USA in 2000.

Space for calculation.

_____ : _____
Europe : USA

1

Marks | KU | PS

7. An investigation into the effect of a digestive enzyme on starch was set up as shown below.

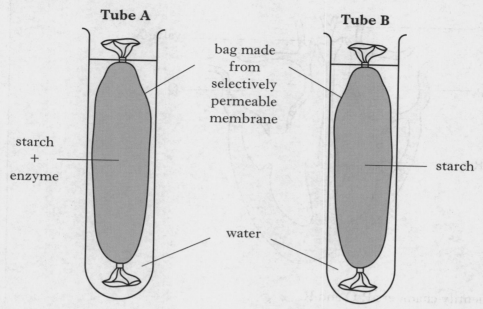

Tube A   **Tube B**

bag made
from
selectively
permeable
membrane

starch
+
enzyme

starch

water

The water from the two tubes was tested for the presence of starch and sugar at the start of the investigation. All the results were negative.

After 20 minutes the water from Tube A gave a positive result for sugar. The other results were negative.

The same results were obtained after 40 minutes.

(a) Complete the following table of results for the investigation.

Time (minutes)	Water in Tube A		Water in Tube B	
	sugar	starch	sugar	starch
0	absent			
	present			

2

(b) (i) Explain why sugar was present in the water in Tube A.

_____

_____

1

(ii) By referring to the size of starch and sugar molecules explain why sugar was found in the water of Tube A.

_____

_____

1

8. (*a*) The diagram shows a section through the heart of a mammal.

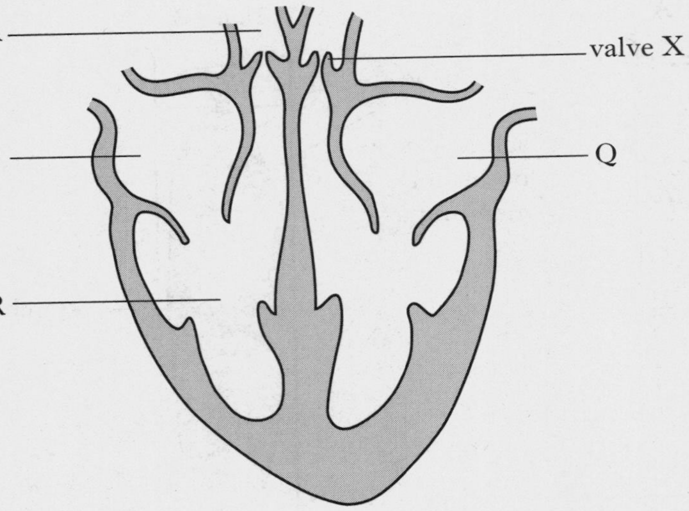

blood vessel A ——————— valve X

P ——————— Q

R ———————

(i) Identify chambers P, Q and R.

P _____

Q _____

R _____

2

(ii) State the function of valve X and name the blood vessel in which it is found.

Function _____

_____

1

Blood vessel _____

1

(iii) Which one of the following statements is correct for blood vessel A?

Tick (✓) the correct box

It is a vein carrying blood to the lungs ☐

It is an artery carrying blood to the lungs ☐

It is a vein carrying blood to the body ☐

It is an artery carrying blood to the body ☐

1

DO NOT
WRITE IN
THIS
MARGIN

Marks | KU | PS

8. **(continued)**

(b) Blood is made of a liquid called plasma which contains red and white cells.

(i) What is the main function of the red blood cells?

_____

1

(ii) State **one** function of plasma.

_____

1

(c) Name the blood vessel that carries oxygen to the heart muscle.

_____

1

[Turn over

9. The pie chart shows the proportions of injuries resulting from different sports recorded at a sports injury clinic.

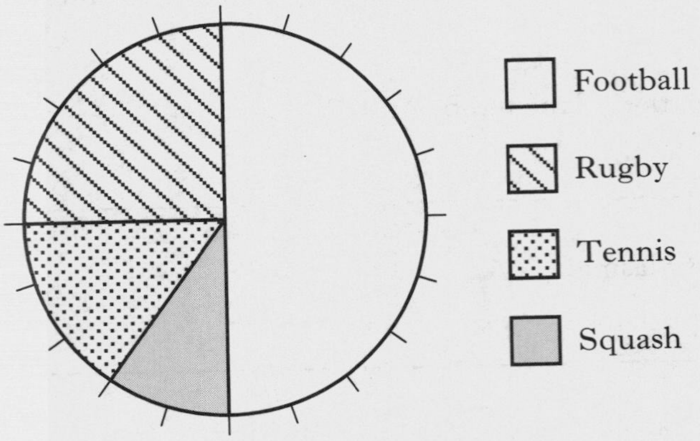

Football

Rugby

Tennis

Squash

(a) Which **one** of the following statements is correct?

Tick (✓) the correct box

More people were injured playing squash than tennis ☐

More people were injured playing rugby than football ☐

Fewer people were injured playing squash than rugby ☐

Fewer people were injured playing football than tennis ☐

1

(b) Which sport resulted in 15% of the total injuries?

_____

1

(c) The number of injuries from playing squash was 32.
How many injuries resulted from playing rugby?
Space for calculation.

_____

1

10. (*a*) Water regulation involves a balance of gains and losses.

Give **one** method of water gain and **one** method of water loss in a mammal.

Water gain _____

Water loss _____

(*b*) The diagram shows the urinary system of a human.

Name structures W, X and Y on the diagram.

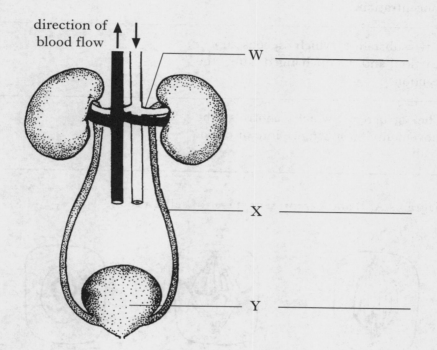

direction of
blood flow

W _____

X _____

Y _____

(*c*) Underline **one** alternative in each bracket to make the sentence correct.

Kidneys produce urine by $\left\{ \begin{array}{l} \text{filtration} \\ \text{absorption} \end{array} \right\}$ of blood and the $\left\{ \begin{array}{l} \text{osmosis} \\ \text{reabsorption} \end{array} \right\}$

of useful substances such as $\left\{ \begin{array}{l} \text{glucose} \\ \text{oxygen} \end{array} \right\}$.

(*d*) Other than water and salt, name a waste product that is removed from the body in the urine.

_____

Marks KU PS

1

2

2

1

[Turn over

11. (a) Complete the table by entering the correct word for each description.

Description	Word
A substance used to make cell structures show up more clearly under a microscope.	
The movement of a substance from a high concentration to a lower concentration.	
Any substance which speeds up a reaction and is unchanged after the reaction.	
The structure which controls the movement of a substance into or out of a cell.	

3

(b) Diagrams A, B and C represent stages of cell division.

A   B   C

(i) Add the letters A, B and C to the empty cells below to show the correct order in which they occur.

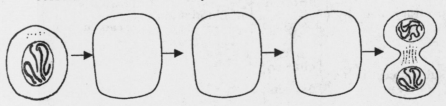

1

(ii) What name is given to this process?

_____

1

12. Vaccinations are given to protect people from diseases caused by micro-organisms.

The following table gives information about some vaccines.

Vaccine	Time vaccine is effective (years)	Booster vaccine required within effective period	Method of vaccination
Hepatitis A	10	yes	injection
Hepatitis B	5	no	injection
Meningitis	5	no	injection
Polio	10	no	by mouth
Rabies	2	no	injection
Tetanus	10	no	injection
Typhoid	3	no	injection

(a) Which vaccine is effective for the shortest time?

_____

1

(b) Which vaccine requires a booster to be given within the effective period?

_____

1

(c) Which vaccine is effective for 10 years, is given by injection and does not require a booster to be given?

_____

1

(d) List all the information which can be obtained from the table about the meningitis vaccine.

_____

_____

_____

1

13. The dental formula of an animal describes the number of each type of tooth on the upper and lower jaw of one side of its mouth.

The diagram explains the dental formula for an adult human.

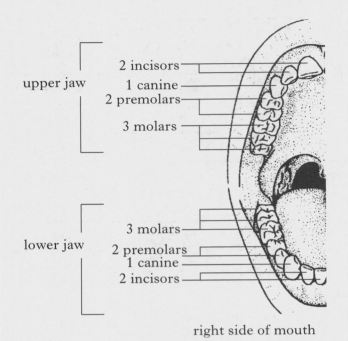

upper jaw

2 incisors
1 canine
2 premolars

3 molars

lower jaw

3 molars
2 premolars
1 canine
2 incisors

right side of mouth

Dental formula = incisors (I)$\frac{2}{2}$, canine (C)$\frac{1}{1}$, premolars (P)$\frac{2}{2}$, molars (M)$\frac{3}{3}$ = 16

Total number of teeth = $16 \times 2 = 32$

The table below gives the dental formulae for some animals.

Animal	Dental formula				Total number of teeth
Dog	I$\frac{3}{3}$	C$\frac{1}{1}$	P$\frac{4}{4}$	M$\frac{2}{3}$	42
Sheep	I$\frac{0}{3}$	C$\frac{0}{1}$	P$\frac{3}{3}$	M$\frac{3}{3}$	32
Rabbit	I$\frac{2}{1}$	C$\frac{0}{0}$	P$\frac{3}{2}$	M$\frac{3}{3}$	

(a) (i) Complete the table to show the total number of teeth for a rabbit.   1

     (ii) Which animal in the table has only 2 canine teeth?

_____   1

DO NOT WRITE IN THIS MARGIN

Marks	KU	PS

13. (continued)

(*b*) A puppy has a total of 12 incisor, 4 canine, 12 premolar and 0 molar teeth evenly distributed between the upper and lower jaws.

Complete the following dental formula for a puppy.

I——— C——— P——— M——— **1**

[Turn over

14. Read the following passage and answer the questions based on it.

The term "raptor" refers to birds of prey. This group includes diurnal types (such as hawks, eagles, falcons and vultures) which feed in daylight. It also includes nocturnal types (such as owls) which feed mostly at night.

With the exception of the vultures, which feed on the leftovers other hunters leave behind, all of the raptors use their feet to catch and kill their prey. Many falcons have an elongated middle toe which they wrap around the prey while still in flight. Hawks' feet have a ratchet-like mechanism to aid capturing and holding their prey without too much exertion. Once the toes and talons have tightened around the prey, they remain locked in place without further effort.

Raptors are completely carnivorous, obtaining all of their required nutrients from their prey. The nutrients which normally come from vegetable matter are often found in the stomachs of their prey. A lot of the water required for survival is also extracted from the prey. Raptors devour the prey entirely, regurgitating the indigestible matter in pellet form once or twice a day.

All of the raptors have hook-tipped beaks which are used for ripping the dead prey. Falcons have a notch on each side of the upper beak forming a tooth-like projection, while some hawks have a more prominent hooked tip to the beak, probably for a similar reason. Vultures have developed a much larger, stronger beak for tearing the hides of dead animals and cracking their bones.

(a) Describe the main difference, mentioned in the passage, between hawks and owls.

_____   1

(b) Describe the feeding habits of vultures which make them different from other raptors.

_____   1

(c) Explain how raptors can obtain vitamins and minerals found only in plants, even though they are entirely carnivorous.

_____   1

(d) Describe **two** differences mentioned in the passage between falcons and hawks.

1 Falcons _____

    Hawks _____

2 Falcons _____

    Hawks _____   2

Marks | KU | PS

15. (a) The table contains information about an experimental cross involving coat colour of mice. The original parents were both true breeding.

	Symbol	Phenotypes	
Parents		brown × white	
First generation of offspring			
Second generation of offspring		75% brown	25% white

Complete the table to show:

   (i) the symbols used for each generation;   **2**

   (ii) the coat colour(s) of the first generation of offspring.   **1**

(b) Decide if each of the following statements is **True** or **False** and tick (✓) the appropriate box.

If the statement is **False**, write the correct word in the **Correction** box to replace the word underlined in the statement.

Statement	True	False	Correction
Information about the forms of a gene in an individual is called the <u>genotype</u>.			
In the nucleus of a cell each gene is part of a <u>characteristic</u>.			
Cells which carry only one form of a gene to the offspring are called <u>embryos</u>.			

3

[Turn over

Marks | KU | PS

16. (a) An investigation of the effect of pH on the enzyme trypsin was carried out. Trypsin solution was added to cloudy suspensions of protein at different pH values.

The suspension became clear as the protein was digested.

The time taken for the suspension to become clear at each pH value is shown in the table.

pH	8·0	8·5	9·0	9·5	10·0	10·5
Time to clear (minutes)	9	4	7	15	30	50

  (i) Use the results from the table to complete the line graph by:

  1 labelling the vertical axis;   **1**

  2 adding a scale for the vertical axis;   **1**

  3 completing the graph.   **1**

  (Additional graph paper, if required, will be found on page 27.)

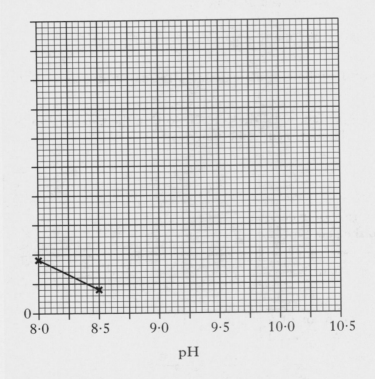

pH

  (ii) Describe the effect of increasing the pH on the time for the suspension to clear.

  _____

  _____   **2**

Marks | KU | PS

16. (continued)

(b) Complete the following sentences by <u>underlining</u> the correct option in each bracket.

Pepsin works best at pH $\begin{Bmatrix} 3 \\ 7 \\ 11 \end{Bmatrix}$ which is $\begin{Bmatrix} \text{acidic} \\ \text{neutral} \\ \text{alkaline} \end{Bmatrix}$.

1

Catalase works best at pH $\begin{Bmatrix} 3 \\ 7 \\ 11 \end{Bmatrix}$ which is $\begin{Bmatrix} \text{acidic} \\ \text{neutral} \\ \text{alkaline} \end{Bmatrix}$.

1

(c) Name the substance from which all enzymes are made.

_____

1

[Turn over

Marks KU PS

17. (a) What is meant by the term "antibiotic"?

_____

1

(b) The table shows the results of treating an infection in cows with various antibiotics.

Antibiotic treatment	Number of cows treated	Number of cows cured	Percentage of cows cured
no antibiotic	2011	1450	72
Amoxicillin	56	48	86
Cephapirin	18	16	89
Cloxacillin	33	25	76
Erythromycin	8	6	75
Penicillin	25	17	68

(i) Why is it better to use the percentages of cows cured rather than the actual numbers cured when drawing conclusions from the results?

_____

1

(ii) The researchers stated that the results for erythromycin were not reliable. Why is this so?

_____

1

(iii) Which antibiotic was the most successful treatment for this infection?

_____

1

(iv) What conclusion can be drawn by comparing the results of the treatment with penicillin to the control group?

_____

1

17. **(b)** **(continued)**

(v) Use the information in the table to complete the bar chart to show the percentage of cows cured by:

1   labelling the vertical axis;   **1**

2   adding a scale to the vertical axis;   **1**

3   completing the bars.   **1**

(Additional graph paper, if required, will be found on page 27.)

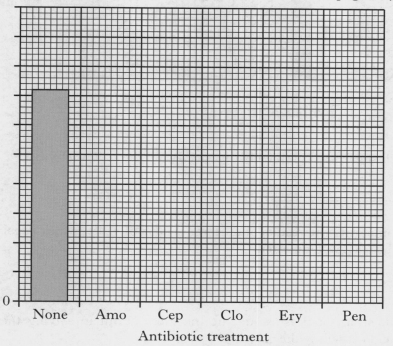

Antibiotic treatment

[Turn over

DO NOT WRITE IN THIS MARGIN

Marks KU PS

18. (*a*) When greenfly feed on cotton plants, they release a sticky mixture of sugars onto the leaves. This causes problems in the cotton industry. Researchers tested three wild yeasts to find a strain which could digest and remove the sugars without harming the cotton plants.

The results are shown on the chart below.

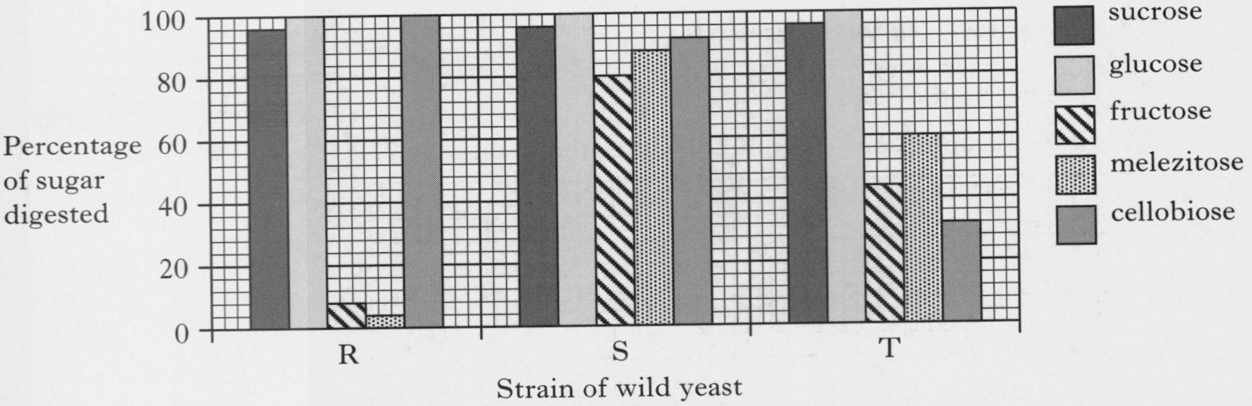

(i) Which sugar was completely digested by all the strains of yeast? **1**

____

(ii) By comparing the results of all three strains of yeast, which sugar was the least well digested? **1**

____

(iii) Which strain of yeast would be the most useful in solving the problem caused by the greenfly?

Give a reason for your answer.

Strain __________

Reason ____ **1**

(*b*) (i) What type of micro-organism is yeast? **1**

____

(ii) Yeast is important in making bread and beer through the process of fermentation.

State why yeast is required in each case.

Bread ____

Beer ____ **2**

DO NOT WRITE IN THIS MARGIN

Marks | KU | PS

18. **(continued)**

(c) (i) Name the type of micro-organism used in the manufacture of yoghurt from milk.

_____

1

(ii) Explain why containers are sterilised before being used for making yoghurt.

_____

1

(d) Micro-organisms carry out fermentation of the sugars in milk. What effect does this have on the milk?

_____

1

[Turn over

19. The meadow brown butterfly shows variation in wing pattern. There are different numbers of black spots on the underside of the hind wings.

The table shows the number of wing spots in a Scottish population of the butterflies.

Number of spots on hind wing	0	1	2	3
Percentage of population	60	20	15	5

(a) (i) Is the variation in the number of spots on the hind wing continuous or discontinuous?

_____

1

(ii) Use the table to complete the pie chart below.

(An additional chart, if required, will be found on page 28.)

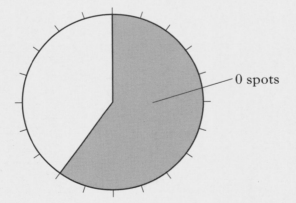

0 spots

2

(b) It has been suggested that the variation in meadow brown butterflies could mean that they come from different species.

What evidence would be required to show that these butterflies all belong to the same species?

_____

1

[END OF QUESTION PAPER]

SPACE FOR ANSWERS
AND FOR ROUGH WORKING

ADDITIONAL GRAPH PAPER FOR QUESTION 16(a)(i)

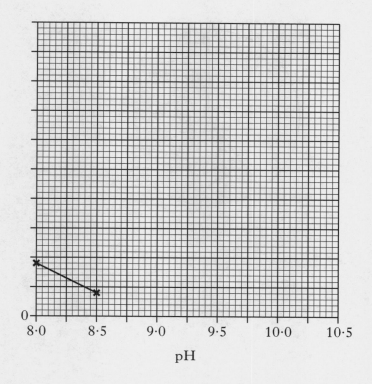

pH

ADDITIONAL GRAPH PAPER FOR QUESTION 17(b)(v)

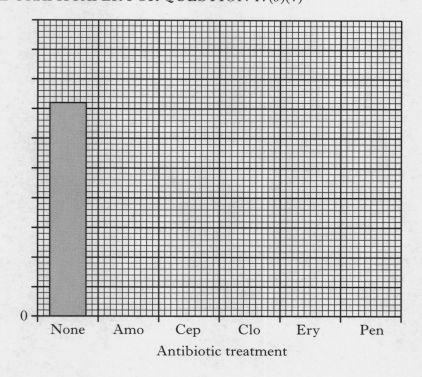

Antibiotic treatment

SPACE FOR ANSWERS
AND FOR ROUGH WORKING

ADDITIONAL CHART FOR QUESTION 19(*a*)(ii)

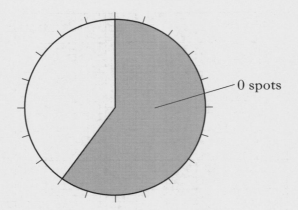

0 spots

SPACE FOR ANSWERS
AND FOR ROUGH WORKING

SPACE FOR ANSWERS
AND FOR ROUGH WORKING

[BLANK PAGE]

[BLANK PAGE]

[BLANK PAGE]

[BLANK PAGE]

[BLANK PAGE]

Acknowledgements

Leckie & Leckie is grateful to the copyright holders, as credited, for permission to use their material:

The following companies have very generously given permission to reproduce their copyright material free of charge: The Herald for the article 'Stirring Stuff's in the Bag' (2004 paper p 16).